Making It Happen

By

Charmie Stewart

ISBN: 1-4107-6298-X (e-book)
ISBN: 1-4107-6299-8 (Paperback)

This book is printed on acid free paper.

1stBooks - rev. 09/23/03

Dedication

This book is dedicated to my brother, Barry L. Stewart.

With positive energy and a strong sense of direction, Barry, you will fly as high or even higher than your favorite basketball star, the amazing Air-highness himself, Michael Jordan.

I've watched you grow and go through so many changes. Yes, it was you who inspired me to write books about the youth's universe. You are my shining star on earth. I love you unconditionally, and although you've made it halfway through your struggles with teen-hood, it does not mean entering manhood gets any easier. There is not a perfect human on this earth. I encourage you to learn from your mistakes. You take your mistakes and turn them all into incredible triumphs. Continue to respect and love all human beings. I pray that you are strong enough to walk away from negative issues, like violence and bad decisions that will come along with pressure from your peers. Stay focused on being a humble, faithful child of God first, and trust me, everything else will come to you in due time. You are going to be an incredible man, I just know it, and as the band Rare Essence says… "Keep pushin'." I love you, my little Father-boy.

To my fellow achievers…

I would like to thank you. I really appreciate your support as well as your unique and selective reading options. My novels are written to inspire young people to expand their abilities and overcome peer pressure. After reading this book, I hope you will walk away with the strength and courage to be a leader, not a follower. As a child, your job is to attend school. Leave the bills and financial responsibilities to the adults. Don't worry about making money while you are attending school. Let yourself enjoy being young. Do not rush what should be the best years of your life. Being a young person these days can be a total drag, especially when everything appears to be wrong in another person's eyes. If you want to achieve and be better than your ego…

- Explain yourself. Help your parents, teachers, and friends understand who you are.

- Sometimes it's better to hear the negative views about yourself from someone else, only because you can always explain your point and oppose what they have to say. Later, both ways can turn into understanding and agreeable corners. That's called "having an opinion." No one wants to be put down. Check yourself before you start checking others who are checking you. They may just have a point.

- Know who you are. Do not pretend to be bad, tuff, smart, or in some cases, even dumb. After all, this is your life. If you don't care, you should start trying. When people see that you are willing to make a change in order to better yourself, they will show you respect, and may even feel comfortable about asking your opinions on certain issues.

- Do not limit yourself. Keep reaching to achieve different heights of success every day.
- Surround yourself with you. When you like yourself, how hard is it for others to like you? You must start somewhere; those who like being around you are basically those whom you enjoy being around.
- We are not batteries. Sometimes connecting negative and positive simply does not work.

So please stay focused and remain positive; and success will remain with you as long as you are faithful and true to yourself and others. Good luck, and may God bless you all.

Introduction

Growing up in the heart of southeast Washington D.C., a person must learn street tactics to survive. D.C., also known as the "Chocolate City", is the home of one of the most well respected presidents, who proved that even a world leader is not perfect. This president will always be remembered for these two famous phrases: "I did not inhale", and "I did not have sexual relations with that woman". This accepting city has proven that yes, there is power in the people. It openly accepted a mayor who was charged with a serious felony to operate once again the District of Columbia. This goes to show you that if you are accurate with what you do in life, no one and nothing can ever stop you from achieving or realizing your dreams. As a reader, I encourage you to pay close attention and try to envision each character in this novel as I tell you the story of three teenage girls who could have been success stories, instead of statistics. Picture their lives as they succeed, and suddenly fail due to their misguided choices.

The message from me to you is this: nothing in life will come to you freely. There's a price to pay for all issues, and everyone must live and learn to survive. There comes a time in life when things seem worse than they really are. Do not give up. You have what it takes to overcome failure. You, and only you must, "Make It Happen".

M.I.H.

The building everyone called eight-seventy was filled with addicts roaming in and out of apartment units. The users rushed to the dealers with haste, waiting their turn to purchase their morning's fix. At the top of the staircase stood a tall, dark-skinned teenage girl who had also been impatiently waiting. Every five minutes, Renée would glance through the apartment building's smeared windows to see if her ride had arrived to take her to school. Renée Butler was her name, but she preferred that people call her Co–Co, because of her flawless dark skin. To an average visitor the loud noises of doors slamming and music blasting throughout the entire building would certainly have been an outrage, but to the people who lived there it was part of everyday life.

Although Co–Co lived in this environment, she had a much different view of her surroundings. She believed her neighbors were lost, and she sometimes felt sorry for the way they chose to live their lives. There were also times when she didn't think of her surroundings as an outrage. She thought her neighbors were living as they thought human residents of an urban area should live. She wanted to be counted amongst the best of the successful former neighbors, who had moved on to quiet and comfortable neighborhoods, for she had been through much tragedy as a child. She lost both of her parents at the age of only eight months; her elderly grandparents and two aunts, who had terrible histories of committing illegal crimes to support their drug habits, raised her. She also had two uncles, one whom she had never met because he was sentenced to twenty-five years to life without parole for killing two people; and her mother's twin brother, who was always on the go, and had no time to spend with her. He was a popular drug dealer who took care of her financially. He made sure she had top-of-the-line designer shoes, clothing, and that her hair and nails were done on a regular basis. She was aware of what he did for a living, but there was nothing she could say to a grown man who took care of his parents, didn't have any children, and was riding high as the "Bill Gates" of the neighborhood.

As time went by, things became worse for the dreamy-eyed teen. At the age of thirteen, her grandmother died from lung cancer, and by the time she was sixteen she had witnessed neighborhood killings, and had helped her elderly grandfather bury two of his children, both within a one year time frame. There seemed to be no end to these harsh, sad stories for the senior high school girl. Although her heart was heavy from the deaths of her family members, she managed to remain strong and eager to attend college as soon as she finished high school.

Co–Co attended one of the toughest high schools in the southeast area of D.C. Although it was overcrowded and very uncomfortable at times, she managed to achieve perfect attendance, not to mention the honor roll each year. This was remarkable, considering her background and family history. She thought about selling drugs a few times, when her uncle wouldn't give her the things she'd ask for when she wanted them. But, she always turned down the opportunities when they presented themselves. One day her friend Vicki, a popular teen known for stylish looks and flashiness, began a conversation with Renée before entering homeroom class. "What's up, Black?"

"Nothing, Vicki... what's up with you?"

"I didn't think you were going to come back to school so soon, seeing how you just buried your Uncle Gary and all", Vicki said. She continued to ask Co–Co questions about the murder of her uncle. When she saw the questions were becoming annoying, she began to ease up a little, and apologized for not showing up at the funeral. "I'm sorry I wasn't able to attend the service, Black." Her voice began to crack as she turned to Co–Co and placed her hand on her shoulder. With a shaky voice, she assured her that if she needed anything, all she had to do was let her know, and she would be there for her.

Co–Co responded with a nod, and hesitated for a minute as the two girls headed toward the stairwell for class, but quickly turned toward Vicki and said, "Hey, there is something I think you might be able to help me with, Vicki. I know you know how to sling that stuff, and I was wondering if you would like to be my partner, because I'm going to need some help. I can't trust anybody else so—"

"What stuff? I mean where did you get it?" Vicki whispered, as she pulled her friend to the side to allow the other students to pass them as they talked.

Co–Co glanced at her watch and gently pulled away from Vicki. "I'll tell you all about it later. Trust me, I will tell you everything."

Vicki was very puzzled. She couldn't believe Co–Co was thinking about hustling drugs. Vicki knew all about selling narcotics, and had the connections to get weight from different parts of town. It seemed strange that she couldn't buy anything because of a current shortage, yet her buddy, who was new to the game, had a plan to get her pockets phat. All she could do was wonder exactly whom or where she got it from. The boggle-brained young girl shook the thought to the back of her mind, and proceeded to class.

5

During one of her classes, Co–Co began pondering the conversation she and her Uncle Gary had had about the death of her parents. He told her exactly what had happened to her mom. Her boyfriend, Co–Co's father, abused her mother. The couple fought and argued about everything. One night Gloria, Co–Co's mother, decided to stay out all night. The next day when she returned, Co–Co's father began beating on her. "She was found in the middle of the bedroom with several stab wounds in her chest and stomach area. He killed himself after stabbing Gloria to death, leaving you, an eight–month–old baby girl, behind." As his voice slowly faded away, Co–Co became aware of her surrounding classmates.

"Renée!" a raspy voice shouted, "Are you all right? Do you need some air?" The concerned teacher walked over, extended her hand toward the young girl's shoulder, and assured her she was available for conversation, if Renée needed it. Mrs. Tipton could clearly see the pain and confusion in the young girl's eyes; and through it all, she was amazed at how Renée remained as strong as she had. She was delighted to see her strong-willed student attend her class every day, although hurt seemed to follow her wherever she went. However, Mrs. Tipton was concerned that soon Renée's family problems would affect her interest in education. She worried that she would drop out, or adopt an "I don't care" attitude, as her other students with family problems had done. Fortunately, she was wrong about Co–Co. Renée never complained or consulted her about anything, except questions concerning class assignments. As a teacher, Mrs. Tipton didn't want to cross the line, so she respected Renée's strength while offering comfort as well. After all, Renée was dealing with serious issues that would affect her adult life. She wanted to help the courageous teen prepare.

The bell rang, and class was over. After daydreaming half the class away, Co–Co stood proudly, as if someone had given her a "be strong, hold on" pep talk. Although Co–Co refused her concerned teacher's sympathy, she appreciated having someone show interest in her feelings, rather than curiosity about the details of what was going on with her and her family.

Walking through the hallways to classes was sort of a relaxation period for Co–Co. She would greet and joke with her fellow schoolmates and teachers as she made her way to her other classes. Like Vicki, she too, was popular. She had an awesome personality, and she didn't have a shy bone in her body. There were days when Co–Co would sing silly skits about television commercials in front of a hallway full of students. She kept the teachers and students laughing all the time. Making jokes and acting silly was a great way to clear her head of the tragic problems from her past. She didn't want people to feel sorry for her at all. Her objective was to show her peers that she was all right, and she wasn't going to make any excuses. She could deal with whatever came her way. At times she felt as if a huge magnifying glass followed her around, because everybody talked about what had happened to her parents, as well as her grandmother, the death of one of her aunts, and her uncle's tragedy too.

Somehow, Co–Co managed to maintain her composure despite her sorrows, and she focused on school and only school. What amazed others most was how determined and eager she was to make something of her life. Co–Co didn't want to be a "family background" teen statistic, so she used all of her positive actions and strong courage to overcome her sadness and hurt. She really impressed her teachers, and the parents who knew the history of her family, especially the ones who had doubts about her character. There were a few who said she was going to run all over her grandfather because her Uncle Gary was dead. Obviously they didn't know her at all because she proved them all wrong. In her mind she knew she had to strive for success, because many people were waiting for her to follow in her other family member's footsteps. She felt that if she did the opposite of what they had done, she would have a chance of becoming a college student. So she studied hard, did well, and continued to focus on being smarter than the day before. Sometimes she would sit and visualize just how excited her grandfather would be on the day of her graduation. She would picture him crying tears of joy, and thanking her for doing what none of his own children had ever accomplished, which was graduate from high school. Co–Co was mature enough to understand the trials and tribulations her grandfather had to face every day. She felt she owed him a true moment of success, and she knew if she dropped out of school her chances would be zero.

Time passed and the final bell rang, signaling that school was finally over for the day. As the hallways began to flood with excited teenagers, a loud voice shouted, "Hey, Black." It was Vicki calling Co–Co by the personal nickname she had given her. She signaled to Co–Co to head toward her locker. "Now, what were you saying about getting rid of some stuff?" she asked, as she proceeded to open her locker.

"Yeah…" Co–Co replied. She kept her voice to a murmur, so no one could hear what they were talking about. "Listen, when my Uncle Gary was murdered, I went through his things, hoping to find some nice jewelry and a few pieces of designer clothing that I could keep for myself. I ended up keeping everything except his shoes. I gave those to my granddaddy. Anyway, I was going through everything, and I found a long list with the names of all the people who owed him money, and a few nasty pictures of some of the girls from around the way. I started going through his drawers and—"

"Yeah, yeah, yeah," Vicki said impatiently, as she swayed her hand in a circular motion. "Tell me about the stuff. How much did you find?"

Co–Co began to frown; she didn't like the way her friend rudely interrupted her story. "Hold on, dag, let me finish," Co–Co demanded. "When I opened the drawer, I noticed it was empty, so I reached my hand inside the dresser. That's when I came across these block-shaped packages with gray duct tape wrapped around them. I removed the drawer from the other side of the dresser, and there were a couple of blocks on that side too. So, tell me how much money I could get for something like that."

Vicki's eyes were about to pop out of her head. "Are you sure you want to do this, Black?" She began

11

to smile, and so did her curious friend. "Do you know what this means? As far as I'm concerned, you are going to be caked up for a while." Vicki grabbed hold of Co–Co as if she were her personal trophy. "C'mon, let's go. I'm going to show you what is what as far as slinging those bricks are concerned, and if this stuff is any good, Black, you are definitely going to be on."

The two girls headed toward the double doors, and as they exited the school building, Co–Co paused. Before taking another step, she remembered she had left one of her books in her locker after being dismissed from seventh-period class. She had been so involved in her conversation with her street-smart friend that she had totally forgotten about her English book, so she jolted back into the building.

With the music blasting from every other car and the sight of trendy teenagers mingling around after school to entertain her, Vicki didn't mind waiting. It wasn't long before she would join the crowd of her fellow schoolmates in a miniature block party. The teens bobbed their heads to a local neighborhood band as the hard sounds of the bass coming from the car stereo systems intoxicated their young minds. They began to slowly bounce and rock from side to side as they sang along with the chorus. "This is how we party in our neighborhood… either way we do it, it's all good." Vicki continued to enjoy herself, and not once did she notice her friend standing behind her. Within seconds Co–Co joined in, and it wasn't long before both of them were having their own personal two-way parade. They danced all the way to Vicki's car, but before they could enter the car, a black Jeep distracted them. The Jeep appeared to have five or six guys in it, and when the driver pulled up too close to Vicki's door, she became a little upset. Before she could open her mouth to speak, a giggly voice carried out across the air, causing Vicki to release an aggravated sighing sound. The laughter came from their friend Shawny.

Shawny was a flirtatious teen who could easily ace the SAT test. She was a very smart, witty girl, but her zealous ways with the neighborhood boys sometimes made her seem as if she couldn't read a book. This was especially true if the young men were good-looking, wore nice clothes, drove the latest model cars or trucks, and had a name for themselves out in the streets. Shawny's confidence came from being a young sex symbol. Her skin was an even melon tone, and she had the shape and curves of a full-grown woman, which attracted many older men to her. From time to time, she could be seen on dates with men in their early twenties. To her, that made her mature. She thought she was untouchable because she had all the high school boys jockeying for her, watching her every move.

Both Co–Co and Vicki knew about the fast lane taken by their promiscuous friend, but who were they to judge her? The girls were close friends, and that was all that mattered. They really didn't care what people thought. Co–Co and Shawny's relationship began before kindergarten. Co-Co's grandmother was Shawny's babysitter until her parents made enough money to move away from the low-income apartment complex, which meant she would have to attend school in Maryland. Shawny somehow convinced her parents to allow her to use a family member's address as proof of residence, because she wanted to continue attending D.C. Public School. Both parents agreed, but only under the condition of her maintaining her grades; which she did, and the two of them had been inseparable ever since. Vicki met Shawny when the girls entered junior high school, and although she hadn't cared too much for her in the beginning, she put up with her presence, and grew to develop a close relationship with her as they became older teenagers. As a matter of fact, one of the main reasons Vicki respected Shawny was because when it came to schoolwork, she really excelled. She tutored Vicki and even Co–Co from time to time. It was true that the girls hated her conceited ways, but they all loved each other as if they were blood-related sisters. They had developed that kind of relationship over the years, and regardless of what people had to say about any of them, they all stuck up for each other.

"Aw… that's messed up, y'all was about to leave me," Shawny cried, as she stood in front of the truck, panting for air.

With a puzzled look on her face, Vicki began questioning her. "What? Are you serious? Why didn't you ask Cuz to give you a ride? You seemed to be enjoying their company before you spotted me and Black getting ready to roll out."

Before giving any explanations, Shawny helped herself into the back seat. "Vicki, you need to stop trying to be my mother all the time, girl. I know how to handle myself, and for your information, Kevin and them were parked in front of the deli, smoking a bob. They asked me if I wanted a hit. I said, 'Nah... but y'all could drop me off around the corner, so I can get a ride home with Vicki and Co–Co; I know they are looking around for me by now" she said, as she gave Vicki a light pluck on the earlobe.

"Hey, aaaah, hold up, Shawny, you're right. She is not your mother. She can't tell you not to get into stolen trucks with those burned–out weed head dudes, who don't care anything about you. I mean, hey, if that's what you like, then Vicki should love it. Why should she care about what is going to happen to you, huh? I mean, after all, hmmm, she's only your friend right?"

"Aw, be quiet, Co–Co, your black butt just had to get your lil comment in, didn't you? Y'all knew what I was trying to do."

There was nothing left for Vicki to say. All she could do was shake her head in disgust at how thoughtless Shawny was for getting into that truck with those boys.

The girls listened to the sounds of Rare Essence, an outstanding group of musicians from the hood, as they made their way around various neighborhoods throughout the District. They passed through all the familiar strips and popular hangout spots, such as Linda Pollin, an enormous apartment complex of white connecting towers, which camouflaged the dealers well as they served the neighborhood fiends hand in hand; Chesapeake Street, an extended neighborhood strip to view the loud children playing in the dirt, and throwing rocks, as the hustlers lounged around in their fold-up chairs, as if they were on vacation. It was also the infamous block where all the females came to court young or old, they were there trying to hook up with a well-dressed thug, Sixth Street, a quiet side street which crossed Chesapeake Street, where the neighborhood gamblers roamed and enjoyed sipping expensive alcohol to comfort their sorrows, after loosing thousands of dollars; Brandywine Street, the boulevard of "the baby momma drama". And the hottest spot of them all, Congress Park, a.k.a. "Da Park", where anything and everything went down day or night. Wherever the ghetto superstars were, Vicki and her hanging partners could be found; and the girls stopped to chat with a few people on their journey home. It seemed that each and every neighborhood was having a block party.

Finally they approached Vicki's apartment complex. It was quiet in her neighborhood and the grounds were kept very nicely, although from time to time someone would come through the complex to purchase crack from Vicki. It was nothing like the neighborhood where Co–Co lived. The complex had five or six buildings, and was one of the cleanest residential neighborhoods in the Southeast area. Many of the popular guys and girls lived in this complex. To most people, it was a luxury to live in the Trenton Place Apartments. Some even thought they were better off than others who lived in different neighborhoods throughout the Southeast area. One of the reasons the buildings were so tidy was because the city didn't own the complex. The residents who lived there could not understand why some of the people from the projects would tear up and destroy the places in which they lived. They would spray paint art on the side of their homes, creating tombstones that read things like "R.I.P. Big–O", or "We Miss you Kay–Kay." In Vicki's complex the only signs visitors were able to read were in bold, black letters on a white metal billboard. One which read, no loitering, and the other implied no standing on the grass.

Vicki lived with her brother K.C., who was her guardian. In the beginning, he and Vicki grew up together under the care of their aunt, who at the time was also raising four children of her own in a two–bedroom apartment near Co–Co's neighborhood.

Vicki's parents were addicts, and it was only a matter of time before the court system would have placed both K.C. and Vicki into the foster homes in the District. Luckily, they had a caring family member to rescue them the night a concerned neighbor complained about them being home without supervision.

K.C. couldn't have been more than four or five years old when that occurred, and although the young boy didn't quite understand what was going on, he knew he wanted to protect his baby sister. From that day on he made sure she was taken care of, whether their parents helped them or not.

K.C. was very grateful that his aunt took them in, and she promised him that as soon as he was grown, and responsible enough to take care of them both, she would give him custody of Vicki. As a teen, he realized his parents were not going to give up the streets for them. He hated being in a two–bedroom apartment with six other people every night, so he went to school, made good grades, and got himself an after–school job so he could begin saving money for an apartment when he finished school. He promised Vicki that one day he would get a good job, and if their aunt gave him permission, he would come back for her and they would live a comfortable life together. Years passed and his promise became a reality. After high school, K.C. enrolled in a computer camp and received numerous certificates and awards. He later obtained a high–paying job that would enable him to share his earnings with his little sister. Legally, Vicki was supposed to reside with their aunt until she turned eighteen; but once K.C. was old enough to support both Vicki and himself, their aunt gave him permission — along with rules and regulations — to raise Vicki. Now K.C. lived the lifestyle of a high–maintenance homosexual.

Vicki showed him the utmost respect and appreciation for being a strong survivor, as well as a responsible person. She thought the world of her big brother, and when times were not so peachy, they were there for each other and lifted one another in spirit. Just as she accepted his lifestyle and respected his choice to be gay, he accepted her lifestyle and knew all about her bad habits of running after that almighty dollar. He hated her dangerous lifestyle, and warned her time after time about selling drugs and bringing large amounts of money into their home. He tried to point out the serious consequences to her if she got caught. Of course, she was young and impressed by nice clothes and the "associates" who were involved in the game, she heard him talking, but she just wasn't listening.

"Vicki, I hope you came home with an attitude to wash clothes, Miss Girl!" K.C. said in a dragging, shy–sounding tone of voice.

Kicking her dress shoes off near the front door, she replied, "C'mon man, leave me alone. I'm going to wash; I need to change my shoes. I'm going over to Co–Co's house for a little while, but I'll wash when I get back."

Standing in the dining room area with his arms crossed and one leg extended in front of the other, he began to smile. "Good, I'm glad that you're not with that lil freaky thang Shawny. I can't stand her hot tail. Before anybody knows it, she is going to be running around here pregnant, and she won't have the slightest idea of who the father of her baby is… and pick those shoes up from in front of that door, girl, what do you think this is?"

Ignoring his command, Vicki laughed under her breath at the comment K.C. had made about Shawny. "Aw, be quiet. Don't be talking about my girl like that. She's all right. You must want to get with her or something." She opened the door and yelled out into the hallway, "K.C. wants Shawny, y'all", and then she immediately ran out the apartment door.

Within seconds, K.C. came charging behind her, and when he got to the door, he yelled down to Vicki, "No I don't… tell her I want to be her stepmother!" After that closing remark, he snapped his finger toward the thin air, and proudly closed his apartment door.

Making her way down the staircase, Vicki cracked a huge smile. She thought her brother was the funniest homosexual in the District. When she returned to her car, she noticed that Shawny was missing. Before she could ask Co–Co anything, she saw her flirtatious friend batting her eyes and smiling at a huge fat boy. Both she and Co-Co knew for sure that Shawny was not interested in him. Shawny was interested in the expensive truck the fat boy was driving.

"Hey Shawny!" an impatient voice rang out, "If you don't want to be left behind, I suggest that you bring your lil butt on over here, girl." Vicki honked the car horn to get Shawny's attention and pointed in the direction of the car.

Pushing her hand in an outward position, Shawny yelled out. "Go ahead, leave me, I'll call y'all later." She continued to chat with her new friend.

Looking in the rear–view mirror as they drove out into the traffic, Vicki began to speak about Shawny's unbelievable actions. "I don't get it. I mean, I just do not understand how this girl could let a car, truck, jewelry, or even a new pair of Timberland boots, turn her out like that. Did you see how big and fat that boy was?" They both started to laugh and Vicki continued, "I'm saying… why let somebody else material things make you that weak? That's probably not his truck, and just like that," she snaps her finger, "she's all, 'Go ahead, I'll call y'all.' Oh, she is such a lil freak."

With a look of disgust upon her face, Co–Co sat there in silence.

Normally, the girls would joy–ride after school before going home, but they had other things to deal with that afternoon, like figuring out what to do with the packages Co–Co had found. When they arrived at Co–Co's apartment, they were greeted with a huge hug from Mr. Jackson, Co–Co's grandfather. He stopped to hold a conversation with Co–Co for a moment, and after informing her of what he expected her to do before hanging out, he gave her a kiss goodbye on the forehead and shouted, "Don't you forget to call me at work, and if I'm not there, Renée, you can always leave me a message."

Co–Co waved goodbye, and proceeded to walk up the stairs. As soon as she opened the door, a note fell down toward the living room carpet. It was the reminder that her grandfather had spoken of earlier.

"Dag, your granddaddy makes sure you get what he has to say, huh?"

"It's not even like that. I'm all he has now, and he just wants to make sure I'm not out there doing anything crazy like the rest of my people were, you know. And besides, he doesn't ask me for much. The only things I have to do are washing the dishes and going to school. I feel like I owe it to him to do the little extra things like cook, clean, and wash clothes; and what really makes him feel good is that he knows where I am. So I guess being protective is his little way of saying that I am special. Plus, when I follow his rules, he lets me stay out a little longer. That's the best thing I love about my grandfather—he is the man, girl." Co–Co made the point that she was responsible very clear. Vicki understood because K.C. was the same in many ways. The reality was that he was her brother, but Mr. Jackson was a father long before he became a grandfather, which gave him a lot more experience with handling a teenager. He had learned how to be a good parent from his mistakes in the past, so the child would be a good child.

Co–Co went into her bedroom and pulled down the shoeboxes that contained the block–shaped packages. When Vicki saw how many packages there were, her eyes began to stretch as wide as a pair of twenty–inch tires. Suddenly the room was filled with silence. After about ten seconds, Vicki began to yell. "Girl... oh my goodness, Black, do you know how much stuff this is? You are going to get paid, girl!" As she continued to examine the wrapped packages, she assured Co–Co that she knew how to do everything. "I can cook it for you. I know how to weigh the packages if you want to break them down, and I can even show you how to stretch it, but you don't need to do that because you have a lot to work with right here."

Co–Co was speechless. She looked totally lost. She didn't have the slightest idea of what her excited friend was talking about. The only thing she was concerned about was getting the money and keeping this secret hidden from everyone, especially her grandfather.

"Listen, I don't understand all of that stretching and cooking mess you are talking about. Just tell me how much money I can get for all of this stuff, girl..." the confused Co–Co yelled out.

Vicki stood there grinning from ear to ear, and proceeded to explain how she could make more money if Co–Co wanted her to break the whole blocks down into ounces and grams.

During her explanation, she began rubbing her fingertips across her thumb, a gesture of having money in her hand. As she began to think out loud, she said with confidence, "Okay, here's the plan. If we sell all six bricks for thirty–five hundred dollars apiece, that will give you...twenty–one thousand dollars. Or you can break them all down, and make more than that if you want to really get your hustle on." Vicki suggested that she call a few people who had been looking for some weight, which was what the girls now had. But before she could dial a digit, Co–Co jumped up to speak. She told Vicki that she did not want people to know anything about her. She wanted to know why they couldn't get rid of everything by themselves. She honestly didn't realize how much stuff they had in their possession. Vicki, on the other hand, was totally aware, and she knew the correct procedures for getting rid of it, so she explained to her clueless friend how selling a few packages worked. She saw how agitated and nervous Co–Co had become, and she knew she had to help her get rid of the drugs immediately.

"Please, Vicki, you have to be smart about this. That's the reason I told you about the packages, and not Shawny. If I wanted people to be in my business, then I could have given her a piece of the action."

With a blank look upon her face, Vicki agreed by nodding her head. She stated that somebody had to know she had been put on, or she had ways of getting in touch with someone who had the weight. So she suggested that she call a guy by the name of Neal to let him know she knew where to get what he needed.

When Vicki noticed that she didn't have his number in her jacket pocket, she went out into the living room to check her backpack, and sure enough, it was there. As she proceeded to dial his telephone number, she whispered, "Watch this."

"Hello, what's up? This is Vicki. Were you still interested in what we talked about the other day, because my man is back now, and he got dat. Okay… how many? Well, let me call him and let him know, and I'll hit you right back."

The deal was done. She made him believe she was the person in the middle of the whole transaction. She was confident about Neal because she had dealt with him before. With confidence, she winked her eye at Co–Co. She told her that she was going to wait a couple of minutes before she gave Neal a call. He said he wanted to buy four packages, which was more than enough money for two teenage girls to spend.

Co–Co asked Vicki how much she would sell each of the packages for, since he was a friend of hers and someone with whom she had done business in the past.

Vicki responded by saying that she was not going to change the price, because there was a coke shortage and no one had it but them at the moment. If she went down in price, it wouldn't be right for her imaginary "big man."

"I'm going to stay at thirty–five apiece. That's about right, and that's also a nice fourteen thousand dollars, girl!"

Once again Co–Co became a little shaky. "What are we going to do with all of that money?"

"I don't know, Black, but I'm sure that we'll find something to do with it!" Vicki laughed at her nervous friend, who didn't have a clue about what she was getting into. Time passed and Vicki made the call. The deal was set up for the next night about nine o'clock in the evening.

Co–Co asked non–stop questions about the guy with whom Vicki was doing business. She wanted to know what type of dude he was, and if he could be trusted after she handed him the stuff.

Vicki tried hard to explain to Co–Co how she had engaged in business with Neal and his brother several times in the past. She told her that he and his brother were the very first ones to give her work back then. "Don't worry, Black, he is cool, and if it bothers you that much, you can come with me to drop off the packages. Trust me you will see that he is all right.

31

He's not going to do anything to me, and besides that, he knows I know a whole lot of people. He certainly doesn't know whose stuff I have, or who's coming with me, not to mention that he is already caked up anyway. Girl, he is probably still spending money from 1989, because he was a baller back in the days."

With a look of doubt upon her face, Co–Co adjusted her lips to the right side of her face and replied, "Oh… '89, huh? Then how come he's still out here slinging? If his money is so long, what is he doing wrong? He should have bought himself a lil business or something. That's dumb. He should be lucky that he's not locked up or dead."

"Aw, shut up, Miss Know–It–All but don't know hustling," Vicki responded as they placed the packages back into the boxes.

Later that evening Co–Co received a call from Shawny. She wanted to know if she and Vicki wanted to go out clubbing with her and a couple of girls from around the neighborhood. Co–Co's first instinct was to tell her no, but she thought to herself, *what would a little bit of fun with Shawny and those wild girls from around the corner hurt?* Nothing, she thought, except her vocal cords from the extreme yelling and hollering that's usually done during a night of clubbing.

Feeling a little unsure of whether to speak for Vicki, she responded in a shaky, uncertain way. "Ah...uh-huh, yeah I guess. I have to call her, and I'll call you back."

After she hung up with Shawny, she immediately phoned Vicki. Unfortunately, she received her answering machine, so she informed her about going to the club with Shawny and her lil clubbing crew from around the way. She also suggested that if Vicki wanted to go, she should give her a call, because she didn't want to ride in the same car as Shawny and her lil 'hood–rat associates.

Co–Co knew that the chances of Vicki checking her messages were very slim. It was Friday, and Vicki was out on the pound getting her hustle on. Co–Co knew she would be ready to go home as soon as she entered the place, if she had to attend the function with Shawny and her friends. Time was flying, and as usual, it was time to call her grandfather at work. They talked for about twenty–five minutes, and before the conversation ended she asked him for permission to hang out with a few of her friends. She knew he wouldn't mind, but being responsible was a top priority with her. She wanted him to feel good and proud that she was able to ask him anything. He trusted her because she earned his trust, and that was a good thing. After hanging up the telephone, she began going through her closet to find an outfit to wear that night.

That night Shawny confirmed with Co–Co that her cousin was going to pick her up around ten–thirty. Co–Co agreed to be ready and headed for the shower. Sure enough, ten–thirty rolled around and it was time to go. Co–Co was decked out from head to toe, decorated in the finest designer gear. Nothing too fancy, but a little too jazzy to wear to Club-U. Club-U was a spot uptown in northwest D.C. By day, it was a busy government building where the mayor and other important officials could be spotted entering or exiting during business hours. By night, the building was surrounded by well–dressed young men and women who came to hear their names and neighborhoods shouted out — what was known as the roll call — by that night's live go–go band. When Shawny's cousin arrived, Co–Co was so shocked by the girl's outfit she had to struggle not to laugh out loud. She couldn't help herself. The girl looked as if she was going to pop at any second. Her boobs were coming out of the tight–fitting blouse she was wearing, not to mention her too–tight jeans. They were so tight her butt was smashed flat, as if someone had chopped her backside completely off. This was not what weakened Co–Co with humor. It was her too–small Gucci sandals which displayed her unpolished toenails. What made it worse was that she found it acceptable to display her huge corns, which were the size of popcorn kernels. As they made their way down the stairs, the girl complimented Co–Co on how cute she looked. Co–Co appreciated the compliment so she thanked her, however, she couldn't reciprocate. Instead she told her that she liked her shoes and inquired about a different color. Once they entered the car they made small talk all the way to

Shawny's house. After picking up Shawny and the other two girls, they were off to the club.

The girls were enjoying themselves, and a lot of familiar faces roamed throughout the place the entire night. Co–Co danced and mingled, and the other girls did the same. It was a perfect night; there was no fighting, and everybody was getting along with one another. Especially Shawny, who bumped into the fat boy who had been driving the Range Rover truck earlier that afternoon. They began a conversation, and from the looks of things, they were getting better acquainted with one another. When the club lights came on, signaling that the band was going to go on a twenty - minute break, it was time for those who had been on the dance floor to mingle and get drinks during the break. Across the room, Co–Co saw Shawny and the fat boy grinding against the wall. She kept her distance, because it wasn't a surprise to see Shawny acting hot and wild.

Co–Co remained mellow and continued to bob her head to the music being played by the P.A. Tech.

When the lights went down, signaling to the crowd that the second half of the show was about to begin, Co–Co made her way toward the entrance of the club. She knew it would be difficult and frustrating to exit after the show was over, because just like every club in every city across the world, people loved to hang around and procrastinate afterwards.

It wasn't long before all of the girls had hooked up to go home, all except Shawny. The girls waited around the club for about fifteen minutes then went searching for her. When they found her, she was sitting in the lobby of the building having a conversation with the plump friend she had made that afternoon. Her cousin was anticipating embarrassing her in front of the guy, because she didn't have enough decency to ask or even inform her, the driver, that she wanted to talk to her friend for a while. Co–Co also became a little agitated. She thought that Shawny was being very inconsiderate.

The tension between Shawny and her cousin was so thick you could have cut it with a steak knife. When Shawny noticed the look on her cousin's face, she immediately began apologizing. She suggested that it was okay to leave her there because she had a ride home. At that point there was nothing else for the girls to do except leave, and as they entered the car they continued to mingle and yell out to people they knew. During the drive home, the girls talked about the good time they all had as well as how rude Shawny had been. By the time Co–Co was dropped off, it was almost two o'clock in the morning, and her grandfather was waiting up for her. Before she could get the key into the door, he opened the door, awaiting her arrival.

"Hey, party-head, did you have a good time?"

With an honest, disappointed look on her face, she said, "No, and I wish I would have stayed home."

Her grandfather headed toward his bedroom, and as he walked past Co–Co, he gave her a soft pluck on top of her head. He assured her that soon she would grow out of having fun, so she had better enjoy every minute of it while she was young and free of bills, not to mention people who would depend on her, like children and grandchildren. "Before you become a responsible adult, Renée, you must experience having fun and being carefree, girl. So the next time you are out with your friends, shoop, shake a leg for granddaddy, 'cause I definitely can't afford to have fun."

Co–Co laughed at her grandfather's ill dance and his funny comment, and as she too made her way to her bedroom, she understood exactly what her grandfather was talking about. For some reason she had that disappointed look pasted on her face. She felt angry with herself because she knew from the start that going out with Shawny and her crew was a bad idea. She wasted no time at all retiring herself. She took a dive into her bed head–first, fully dressed. She didn't even bother to remove her shoes. The next morning she found herself very uncomfortable, and felt quite heavy because she had slept in her clothes from the night before. After removing her clothes and shoes, she continued to lie in bed for a while. A while turned into hours, and once again she was out like a light, until her telephone began to ring. It was Vicki. Right away Co–Co began telling her all about the episode with Shawny and her foul–dressed cousin. The girls were about forty–five minutes into their conversation, exchanging jokes and making silly comments about Shawny and her crew, when they were interrupted by Co–Co's other line, it was Shawny. She was calling to ask another dumb favor.

"Co–Co if my mother calls there, could you tell her that I just left and I'm on my way home? Okay?"

Co–Co was shocked. "I know you did not, tell me that you did not spend the night with that big fat boy, Shawny!" There was silence for a second or two before Co–Co ended the conversation. "Girl, you need to get yourself together. Call me when you get home. Bye." She then clicked off the telephone line.

Of course, by the time Co–Co clicked over to Vicki, she had already hung up. Co–Co called her back to ask her about the plans to get rid of the packages, and Vicki told her she would be over to meet with her later that afternoon. The two girls ended their conversation and decided to prepare for the rest of what looked like a great Saturday around the way.

Later that afternoon, Vicki arrived at Co–Co's house with a smirk upon her face, displaying her huge, deep dimples and her ridged, chipped front tooth. A person would have thought she had won the million–dollar lottery, judging from her happy–go–lucky attitude. After watching television for a few hours, she made the call to meet with Neal. Their conversation was quite short. Basically it was just a call to confirm the place and time of the meeting. When the two girls pulled up, Vicki began beckoning Neal and his brother in their direction. She pretended to have a conversation with her connection on her cellular phone, and as the brothers approached they overheard her saying, "Yeah... they are right here. It's just two of them; Razell and Mark are across the street." She then began making funny faces at the cellular phone. Vicki continued to play the security game by acknowledging Neal while speaking into the cellular phone to her imaginary contact person. "Man don't trip, he is like family. All right... I'll see you when I get there, bye." Finally she flipped her cellular phone up and cracked a crooked smile at them both.

"Man he is trippin'. What's up, y'all?"

Neal and his brother were pleased to hear that she trusted them, and felt comfortable about meeting with them in their area. Although they were alert and focused because they didn't know who or where Razell and Mark were, they knew and understood that Vicki's connection had to be secure with them, too. When the two guys got into the back seat of Vicki's car they quickly made the transaction, and then asked, "Is the weight right on these things?"

Vicki assured them they were probably a few grams over, and after exiting the car, the oldest brother shook Vicki's hand and gave her a kiss on the cheek. "Okay, Shorty… you be careful out here."

Vicki waved her hand into the air as a sign that everything was cool and in the clear. The brothers were familiar with that thumbs up signal, and weren't worried at all, because they were strapped and secure with busting off if they had to. They looked in the direction of where she had gestured, and they continued to look until she cranked up her car. They parted on safe and peaceful terms, and before pulling out of the parking spot. Vicki shouted, "Call me if you need to get that."

With a look of relief on her face, Co–Co watched in the passenger seat rear–view mirror as she and Vicki drove away.

"Oh my goodness gracious, Co–Co, all of this money is yours, Black!" Vicki screamed in a funny, scratchy voice. She was not surprised that her plan had worked, but Co–Co was. Anxiously, Vicki insisted they go somewhere to count all of the money, and then they would have to find somewhere to hide it. She turned to Co–Co and asked if it was safe for her to go home to count it.

Calmly Co–Co eased her seat back and threw her hand over her forehead and said, "I'm not sure if my grandfather is going fishing this week or next Saturday. Let's just go back to my house and if he's there, we will just put the money away and count it later."

When the girls arrived at Co–Co's house they were pleased to see her grandfather wasn't home, so they went into Co–Co's room and proceeded to count the money immediately. After counting the money, Co–Co stood in disbelief. Although her grandparents and her Uncle Gary had spoiled her before all of the tragedies and bad times for her began to unfold, she was not used to having that much money at all. "I can't believe how easy that was," she sighed. She thought hustling was much more complicated than what she had just witnessed, because her Uncle Gary had always talked about the cruddy people involved in that lifestyle, especially the ones whom he dealt with on a regular basis.

"That's why you are supposed to deal specifically with people you really know and trust," Vicki explained. She continued to speak about her experiences when she first started slinging drugs, and how she had witnessed a lot of foul play as a newcomer to the game. "I just hope Gary didn't have a bad product, you know, because if that stuff is some garbage, Neal is going to want all of his money back." Vicki's knowledge of hustling hadn't come easily; she had learned everything on her own. She had been threatened, jumped, and even shot at a couple of times because she once hung around with rowdy youngsters, who stayed in chaos. That was when she wasn't hanging out with Co–Co. It wasn't until all of those young guys and girls began dying and/or going to jail for living what they all called a "thug life" that Vicki woke up and began to see that she could be much better than just the daughter of a couple of addicts. That's when she changed her life around, and started to show a little more respect toward herself. She began to take her schoolwork more seriously, and no matter how late she stayed out to clock those dollars, she did her homework for the next day of class. She dealt with whatever came her way. Everyone who knew her was aware of her walking–dead parents, and they had watched her grow up serving her parents drugs as if they were her neighborhood customers. Having Co–Co as a friend had really helped her stay sane; not to mention humble and very positive, especially when it came to her schoolwork. It was true that her life was very dramatic for a young teenage girl, but somehow she managed to make it through each day without a problem. Vicki sat down near the edge of Co–Co's bed

45

in an Indian–style position. She was not prepared for what Co–Co did next. As she watched Co–Co put away the large amount of money, she saw Co–Co pull the last two packages down from the shelves. "Here, Vic, this is for you. I really don't want to deal with this stuff anymore. I promised my grandfather that I would not turn out like the rest of my family, and if I look at this stuff another day, I know I will just end up flushing it or something."

With a look of surprise written upon her face, Vicki sprang from the floor and asked Co–Co if she was sure that she wanted to do what she had done. "You don't have to give me this, Black, I'm all right. I know you have plans to go away for school, and if you need me to push those last two for you, I will. You don't have to give me anything."

Nodding her head yes, Co–Co insisted that if Vicki didn't take the packages, she would honestly flush them down the toilet. She felt very ashamed about what she had done; it was something that she had never done in her lifetime. She had even found a way to contradict herself into believing that it was wrong to sell drugs, but selling drugs would help her get a few things she needed. She had figured it was okay because it was a one–time deal.

Vicki decided to take the two packages, and she asked Co–Co what she was going to do with all of that money.

"This money is going with me when I go off to college, and in a few days, I'm going to pretend I've found my uncle Gary's stash spot, and I'll just tell my granddaddy about the stash and give some of the money to him." Co–Co said as she smiled and nodded her head up and down with confidence. When she asked Vicki what she was going to do with her money, they looked at each other and yelled, "Shopping!"

Everything was going well for them. Co–Co had gotten rid of the drugs and had enough money to survive for at least the first semester or two in college. Vicki was pleased with the fact that she had money in her pockets and money on the way, soon to come from those two packages Co–Co had given her, not to mention the extra money on the street owed to her by addicts.

After getting the room back in order, the girls decided to hang around the house and watch television for a while. Time passed, and there was a knock on the door.

"Who is it?" Co–Co shouted, as she tip–toed to look through the peephole. With one hand on the top lock she asked the question again. A low, silly voice yelled out, "Open the door girl, it's me."

It was Shawny, pretending to be an old lady. Co–Co opened the door and Shawny stepped into the apartment. "What's up y'all, are we going to D.C. Live tonight, or what?" She continued to make her way to the end of the sofa, grinning from ear to ear as she plopped herself down next to Vicki.

"What are all of those goofy looks about, Shawny?" Vicki asked.

"Nothing," she said as she continued to smile and make silly little noises while mumbling under her breath.

"Oh, I know exactly why she is smiling. She spent the night with that big ole fat boy last night... that's why she's smiling," Co–Co explained as she frowned with disgust. Co–Co went on to say that she would not go out with Shawny again. "You are out of your mind if you think you can have me waiting around for you twice. I'd rather party with Grandpa Jackson and his crew at the Chateau's Oldie but Goodie Club on Benning Road before I go out with you again, girl." Shawny waved off her insulting friend, turned in Vicki's direction and asked, "What about you, Vicki?"

Vicki just sat there with a humorous vibe. She was trying to recover from Co–Co's statement about going out with her grandfather. She finally came around and answered, "Nah... I've got something to do tonight, and as a matter of fact, I'm going to get going because I don't want to be out all night." She stood up and continued to laugh at Co–Co as she headed for the door. "I'll see y'all later."

Shawny felt a little stupid after Vicki left the room. "How could you tell her about me spending the night with that boy?"

Co–Co shook her head as if she wanted to say, "Girl, you are pitiful," but instead she lashed out at her. "Shawny, don't even try it, girl. If you are so ashamed of his big butt, then why did you go with him? All I said was that I knew why you were smiling." She headed for the kitchen and Shawny followed her lead. With persistence, she asked again if Co–Co was going to go out with her to the club. Once again the answer was no, and rolling her eyes, Shawny uttered something about how phony Co–Co could be at times.

Unfortunately, Co–Co heard what Shawny had to say, so she stated loudly and clearly as Shawny made her way out the door, "Uh-huh. Just don't call this fake, phony friend the next time you stay out all night, or when you want somebody to lie to your mother again." After yelling into the hallway at Shawny, she slammed the door and made her way to the couch to watch television. Before she could get comfortable, she heard her grandfather's voice in the hall. Every time he tried to turn the lock to get into the apartment, she locked the lock. After trying to open the lock a couple of times, he finally figured out that she was fooling around with the lock on the other side of the door. "Quit playing with the lock, girl!" Co–Co tormented him for just a little while longer, and finally gave in. She tried to get back to the couch as fast as she could, but her timing just wasn't good enough. When he opened the door she was halfway on the couch, playing possum.

"Don't you even try to pretend like you were sleeping, girl, I know that you kept locking that door when I was trying to get in," he said as he headed toward her with his fishing rod and a bucket filled with fish. He went on to say that since she was asleep he should wake her up by placing one of his fish on her head.

Immediately Co–Co jumped up and started to laugh. "Stop playing, Granddaddy, don't do that to me!" He chased her for a second or two, and when he removed his hand from behind his back, it wasn't a fish he held; it was a six–pack of rainbow Trix yogurt. They both started to laugh, and he teased her about how scared and crazy her face was when he began chasing her. The two of them were always pulling

51

practical jokes on each other, and each time they always gave each other a treat or some sort of surprise after the prank was over. They were close, and had a great relationship. After hearing all about her grandfather's fishing trip, a story that seemed to go on for hours, she ended up asleep on the couch in front of the television after all.

On the other side of town, things were looking up for Vicki when she left Co–Co's house. She immediately began planning her road to fast money. Not only was she happy that she would be able to splurge on herself a lot more, she was relieved that she no longer had to worry about owing anyone money, since she had the work herself. On her way home she was greeted by a few of the well–known older guys who had made names for themselves over the years. When the younger crew, such as Vicki and her street colleagues, spoke about them, they sometimes referred to them as the "Old–heads." These were the ghetto superstars who were known for having nice cars, expensive jewelry, and basically a whole lot of respect for being up on their game when it came to the streets. During the spring weather, all of the neighborhood guys would gear up in their local sports apparel. They would purchase embroidered T-shirts, socks, sweatpants, and headbands with logos that spelled out the name of a chain of local urban stores in the D.C. metropolitan area, like ALL DāZ, We R One, MCHUNU, and 4-DEMENTIONS, to name a few.

Although the spring and summer weather brought out a lot of trendy styles, the winter was the best time to view the gear. On every corner in every 'hood there would be a group of guys and girls standing around in nothing but the finest designer sweaters, bearing labels from Coogi, A/X, Gucci, to Iceberg—you name it, they had it. There was no limit when it came to these young hustlers. They wanted to flex their creative styles and dapper ways to impress other guys and girls from other neighborhoods located throughout the City. The amount of money spent on high–priced shoes and leather jackets would sometimes be greater than what some of the residents in the neighborhood paid to rent an apartment.

Unfortunately, appearances didn't affect Vicki at all; she was not impressed by the way the guys looked or dressed. She was what most neighborhood guys considered the "fly, high-maintenance broad." She didn't need a hustler to buy her expensive things; in fact, she had purchased every expensive item she owned. This was her own personal way of rewarding herself for all the hard work she had put in out there on those blocks, selling narcotics everyday. With an independent attitude, there was nothing to dread when it came to wanting or having the best of everything to keep up with the Jones's, even if it meant staying out late to get it. This time around she knew for sure that she was in the game to win, because she had the packages Co–Co had given her, not to mention the money she already had from slinging the week before. Her plans were all falling into place, and one by one, great things would continue to happen for her. Her eyes glistened as she pictured how fantastic things would be for her by graduation day. She knew she had school on Monday, so she had to move fast. The idea was to inform a few people that she had white, uncooked powdered cocaine. After making a few calls, the next thing she would do was take one of the packages of the white powdered substance and create a hard, crystal, rock–like substance. She would later chop the big rock down into various weights in ounces and grams, and then she had to individually bag each of them in clear plastic bags. She would seal each by tying a small knot, and after that she had to neatly cut the excess plastic from the packages. This process was going to take hours, and she was quite focused on making sure that everything was perfect. Time was definitely on her side because she had the house all to herself. K.C. worked a night job during the weekends, and she knew it would be hours before he would be returning home. With that in mind she continued to work at her own sweet little pace, as if she was cooking herself a meal. The telephone rang and she anxiously answered, hoping it was one of her street colleagues inquiring about her hook–up. Unfortunately the call was from Co–Co.

"What's up Vicki? What are you doing?"

"Nothing, I'm just in here cooking up, so I can be ready for tomorrow." Vicki tried to fast–talk Co–Co because she wanted to hurry off the telephone. She constantly rolled her eyes toward the ceiling, praying that Co–Co would soon get her message about cooking up. Unfortunately, Co–Co didn't have the slightest clue of what Vicki was talking about, so she went on and on about anything and everything she wanted to discuss, until Vicki just couldn't take any more conversation.

"Hey, Black, I have to go. I told you that I was cooking up—I will call you later."

"Yeah, right, girl, I know that Oodles of Noodles does not require that much skill. All you have to do is boil water, and drop the dag–on things in the pot."

The girls both laughed, and Vicki stated again that she really had to go. Before hanging up the telephone, she assured Co–Co that she would give her a call later that evening. When she hung up the telephone, she continued to laugh at her clueless friend who thought she was actually cooking food. After preparing her product, she was amazed at how much money she was going to have within a few weeks. If she sold her goods for the exact price without accommodating people who wanted her to accept partial payments until they sold the product later, she would soon be sitting pretty on top of a lot of green street cash.

There was residue all over the countertop, and her kitchen sink was filled with the instruments needed to manufacture what was now crack cocaine. She then gathered all of the neatly wrapped packages, placed them into a large plastic grocery store bag, and hid the drugs in a secure place. The only thing left for her to do was to clean the counters and sterilize the pots and eating utensils she had used to cook the drugs.

While she was cleaning, Vicki's pager went off. When she pressed the button, she began to sigh a little. What she thought was an opportunity to set up a drug transaction wasn't one at all—it was her brother. Instead of calling home first, he had decided to page her, because he automatically thought she would be hanging out on the corner. As always, she returned his call right away to let him know where she was and exactly what her plans were for the rest of the night. From time to time he chastised her just to let her know that although they were siblings, he was the one with the authority. He trusted her, and she felt comfortable about coming to him with all of her problems, no matter the subject. Their relationship was very unique, and their bond became stronger and stronger by the day. In no way was he trying to send her a message that he didn't trust her, because he had great faith in her; however, his conscience bothered him from time to time because he was aware of her lifestyle. Vicki knew he was concerned, and she made it her business to act as if she was just a petty pusher who sold just enough to keep a pair of new shoes on her feet and a few dollars in her pocket. In actuality, she was straight–balling, and making her paper just like the rest of the hustlers out there in the 'hood.

After talking to her brother, Vicki decided to call Co–Co back. The two girls joked and talked about everything from family members to the latest happenings around the 'hood the week before. They went on and on until the subject of school came up.

"Did you know about the test in Mrs. Brown's class on Monday?"

"Yeah, Black, I knew about it. That is why I am returning your call so I can get started on my studying, Miss Thang!"

They both continued to discuss what they thought was going to be on the test, and speculated on who was going to get the best grade. When Vicki made the comment that she really didn't have to study, Co–Co spoke over her voice and stated with confidence. "Oh, you don't? Girl, you better wake up and smell that thing called reality coming. You know good and well that you need to study so stop faking sweetie!"

Shocked at her friend's lack of confidence, Vicki replied, "Whatever. My G.P.A. has been 3.0 since my junior high days, so stop hating on me. As a matter of fact, I just might be the one to walk off the stage with that scholarship in my hand, so stop trippin'."

With smooth–sounding whispers of confidence in her voice, Co–Co replied. "Nah, nah, nah… see baby, my G.P.A. is a hot 4.0, and you're right, you may have that chance of getting hold of that scholarship on graduation. Only, I said *only* if I choose to let you hold it during our photo session after the ceremony is over!"

They both laughed and made fun of each other for another ten minutes or so, and before ending their conversation Co–Co made Vicki promise to pick her up on time for school Monday. Vicki assured her that she wouldn't be late because she had to drop off one of her little cousins at the day care center around the corner from Co–Co's apartment complex early that morning. Sunday came and went, and things were basically the same for all three of the girls. Shawny was out on a Sunday night movie date, Vicki was out on the pound getting her loot right, and Co–Co was at home with her grandfather cooking Sunday dinner and watching television.

The next morning Vicki showed up as promised. Normally Shawny would be standing outside with Co–Co, waiting to get picked up too, but when the girls noticed that she wasn't going to show up, they decided to leave so they wouldn't be late for class. When the girls arrived in front of the schoolhouse, Vicki noticed that their fast–tailed friend was stepping out of an Infinity Q45. It wasn't long before Vicki gained the attention of Co–Co by clearing her throat and pointing her head in Shawny's direction "Uh-um... look at your girl over there, just flexing!" Vicki continued to make small jokes to Co–Co as they both stood there waiting and watching Shawny and her newfound friend on the other side of the street.

"Ooh... y'all are so nosy, why are y'all standing around watching me?" Shawny began to smile and continued to blush as she made her way toward the girls. She went on and on about how she thought she had seen them that morning going to the exact breakfast place she and her friend had gone to. It was obvious she was looking a little too hard, because the girls did not go to get breakfast at all. They both knew what her conversation was really all about. They knew that was Shawny's way of letting them know that her new friend had treated her to breakfast at the infamous Steak n' a Sac Restaurant that morning.

Throwing her hand up toward Shawny's face, Co–Co stated, "Whatever, girl! I'm just glad we didn't decide to wait for you this morning, and the next time you are going to have a ride, we sure hope that you inform a sista' or something!" She then reached out and grabbed both of her friends and led them into the school building. Before the students could make it to their classrooms, a fight broke out in the hallway. Students were running everywhere and the entire student body was in an uproar. It took a while before things were back in order, because the school's security guards had a hard time getting the students to calm down. A number of teachers assisted the guards with instructing the students to report to their assigned classrooms. By the time everyone had settled down, the police had finally arrived, and they proceeded to question the students who were involved. It was later announced that two girls who didn't attend the school at all were involved.

Although Co–Co was there engaging in conversation, her mind drifted off, and she began to wonder exactly how different it was going to be when she got away from those immature, rough and rowdy teens. She shook her head in a disgusted manner and spoke in a depressed tone. Yet she was relieved to know that she was going to achieve her goal of graduating with honors. "Man… I can't wait until I graduate and go away to college. I'm sick and tired of seeing and hearing the stupid nonsense in this school. People just don't have a clue—I mean they just don't get it. All they are doing is making it hard for themselves." There were times when she became frustrated and angry, but not once did she feel the need to act as ignorant as her negative peers did. To her, it really was not all about being bad or hard, because she knew what came along with the reputation. "I know that people look at me the same way they looked at my cousins, aunts, and uncles. So when I hear a story about girls fighting over dudes who probably have other girlfriends somewhere else, it helps me. It lets me know that, hey, Renée, you have got to keep on pushin', don't stop. Bust another A+ in chemistry; try hard to get a certificate or another outstanding award of recognition for doing well."

Co–Co was positive that she was going to be an example of beating the statistics of becoming a young, hot–headed teenager gone bad. Her classmates just sat there with a look of belief in their eyes. They knew she had potential, and as far as accomplishments were concerned, she was way on her way to realizing her future goals. As she spoke, her peers took each and every word seriously. They all agreed and nodded their heads as if they were listening to the sounds of one of the local go–go bands playing a vicious tune, only this time it was the sounds of Co–Co's live dreams, playing out loudly and clearly. When that class was over, she was on her way to another class, when suddenly the sound of heavy breathing and laughter distracted her and made her a little curious. She wanted to find out who was there, so she peeped her head in the direction of the sounds. It was Shawny and one of the guys from the basketball team making out beneath the stairwell entrance.

"Shawny! What is wrong with you, girl?" she shouted, as she made her way over to interrupt them. The couple immediately stopped, as if they had been disturbed by one of their parents. With a look of total embarrassment upon her face, Shawny quickly unwrapped her leg from around the boy's waist. The boy stepped off, making his way toward the staircase, and as Co–Co watched him leave, displayed a big smile. Before climbing the stairs he turned in Shawny's direction and indicated a telephone by placing his thumb near his ear and his pinky near his mouth, then signaled her to call him later. Before she could agree, Co–Co snatched her away, positioning her in the opposite direction. She angrily informed her hot–pants friend that he had a baby on the way. "I hope you don't think he is serious about you Shawny, because he has a baby on the way by that girl Shakima, and if she finds out that you are messing around with him, pregnant or not, she will try to stab you. He is not worth getting cut over!" Co–Co told Shawny she was much better than what everyone thought, then she went on and on about how disrespectful she had become to herself. "You are out of your mind, girl. You need to quit while you still have a little bit of respect going for you. Shawny, I just don't get it. I mean, first you were going with the boy Sean, who you decided to leave alone for his brother Rodney. Then you were with Sean's best friend Fred, and you ended up leaving him for his cousin Lump because he drove a Lexus. What makes this a shameful thing is how they all hang around each other and are still cool with each other, and what makes it even worse is that they all talk bad about you. They even make jokes about how they all had you and what they should have done with you when you slept with them. That's not good, Shawny"

Co–Co was very upset with her promiscuous friend. As they began to climb the stairs she continued to preach and ask questions that Shawny just would not answer. "Girl, the other night you stayed with that fat boy, then you were dropped off by some new dude this morning, who I have never seen before, and now look at you! You and Big Slim down here under the stairwell, kissing and humping like a pair of elementary students. I mean, you were all over somebody else's baby's daddy as if he actually belonged to you. What is going on with you, Shawny? You are smart, sweet, and funny, and I don't need to tell you that you are attractive. In fact, your being so cute is probably why you have so much drama and trouble controlling your hot ways. All I'm saying is that it is not too late for you to change."

Co–Co continued her speech as they made their way through the hallway. Shawny did not say one word. She continued to walk and listen as her concerned friend lectured about her uncontrollable behavior. Feeling quite stupid, not to mention embarrassed about her actions, she calmly said to Co–Co, "I'll talk to you later."

As they parted to attend their classes, all Co–Co could do was shake her head at how disappointing her friend had become. She felt as if she had too much respect and a lot of positive things coming her way in life, and maybe it would be better if she didn't hang around Shawny anymore. She also thought that maybe Shawny felt the same way, which was why she was becoming as hardcore as she was, as far as dealing with all of these different guys was concerned.

Those were just her thoughts, because Shawny honestly didn't feel that way at all. She knew that Co–

Co and Vicki cared about her, and although it was hard for her to express just how much she cared about them, she was very grateful to have them both as friends.

After school, the students hung around to mingle and loiter around the schoolhouse. After standing around and talking a little trash, Vicki spotted Co–Co heading toward her car, and Shawny showed up a few seconds after. As Shawny walked closer to the car, she paused and clearly stated to the two girls that they could go home without her because she had promised one of the teachers that she would assist with the programs for graduation. The two girls thought nothing of her generosity to help out with the programs, because she always helped the school's faculty with their organizations printing programs for upcoming events, which would appear in the student's school newspaper. As they proceeded to enter Vicki's car, Co–Co yelled out to Shawny, "Don't forget to call me tonight because we need to talk."

Shawny nodded her head in agreement and assured Co–Co that she would call her as soon as she got home that evening. She knew that Co–Co was disappointed with her, but if she called her that evening their friendship would be on the rocks because sometimes Co–Co didn't know how to talk to people without making them feel dumb or stupid on the inside.

During the ride home, the girls remained silent. It wasn't long before they arrived in front of Co–Co's apartment building. Before Co–Co had a chance to exit the car, Vicki's pager began sounding off, and it continued to chirp non–stop. Co–Co turned to reach for her backpack, but before closing the car door, she stuck her head back into the passenger side and told her friend to be careful.

Barely paying attention to her concerned friend, Vicki adjusted her head in an upward motion to answer. Not once did she look away from her pager—she constantly pressed her pager button to display the telephone numbers. With confidence in her voice she said, "You better believe it!"

After closing the car door, Co–Co stood on the sidewalk with her lips together. As they merged into a tight, guilty grin, she turned and headed for the apartment building steps.

Back at the schoolhouse all of the after-school program students were leaving school, all except Shawny. She gave her fellow classmates an ultimate impression of being very confused, yet interested, in finding out more information, so she stayed behind and pretended to read the literature promoting the math and science programs. It wasn't long before the classroom was practically empty, and she immediately headed in the direction of her teacher, Mr. Baldwin. He was a short, brown–skinned young man who appeared to be in his late twenties or early thirties, and he was extremely handsome. If it wasn't for his professional attire and his distinctive way with grammar, he could have easily been mistaken for one of the senior students. "Mr. Baldwin, I need help with my skirt. Do you think you could give me a hand?" The flirtatious Shawny asked, as she stood there with an inviting look upon her young teenage face.

"No, girl, not in here," the nervous teacher answered as they both stood there lusting for one another. It was obvious that the two of them had something going on, other than a student–teacher relationship.

From time to time Shawny would make up an excuse for why she couldn't catch a ride with her two friends after school; and because it wasn't unusual for her to attend classes after school hours, her staying late to attend Mr. Baldwin's class did not seem out of the ordinary. So on occasional Mondays and Thursdays, she would sneak away to be with him. Of course, the two of them couldn't be seen leaving the school grounds together, so she left the classroom first. Shawny extended her arm in his direction, displaying an open hand, and he placed the keys to his truck there and told her to make sure that nobody was watching her. He waited five minutes after she left the classroom, and then headed toward the administrative office to hand in a few papers. Basically he was trying to pass time to give Shawny enough time to climb into the back seat and get undressed.

Successful every time, she performed the normal routine she followed each and every time the two of them got together. She hopped into the back of the truck and removed her clothes. Because the truck had black–tinted windows, she didn't have a problem with getting undressed, which made it easy on her. She felt comfortable knowing that no one could see what she was doing inside the truck. Ten minutes went by and she began to wonder what was taking him so long. Normally he would arrive within seconds after she had gotten undressed. There was nothing she could do except wait, so she decided to recline on the back seat and listen to the sounds of the other teachers leaving the parking lot, hoping the next sound she'd hear would be him opening the door. Sure enough, he arrived and she popped up at the sound of his presence. "What took you so long?" She asked.

Calmly, he replied. "Oh… I had to call my wife to find out if she wanted me to bring home anything." He glanced at her young curvy body, and said with a regretful tone of voice, "Damn, I wish I was younger!"

Normally, they would drive to Anacostia Park, a neighborhood recreational area that was usually deserted on weekdays. This time they were so anxious to engage in sex that he just parked the truck in a corner parking spot on school premises. He joined her in the back seat and placed his fingers firmly on her breasts. He began to massage them while giving her a long, slow, tongue kiss, and before engaging in sexual intercourse, he softly whispered, "Baby, are you still on the pill?"

Shawny began kissing his neck and messaging his private parts and answered as she panted for air, "Um–huh, you know that I am."

For such an honorable husband, loving father, and responsible teacher, Mr. Baldwin sure wasn't representing himself too well. Not only was he violating God's law by breaking his marriage vows, but he was committing a serious crime in violating a minor. The couple never looked at things that way; he somehow thought it was perfectly all right to do what he did, and he prayed that no one would ever find out.

73

Shawny was senseless; she didn't have any idea of how much the grown man had to lose if the two of them ever got caught. In fact, when it came to having morals, she was clueless, yet of the three girls she was the only one who hadn't come from a broken home. Both of her parents graduated, had good jobs, continued to stay married, and provided well for her, doing everything they could to make her happy. Unfortunately, communicating with her parents about sex was not one of Shawny's strong subjects.

She had lied to Mr. Baldwin; she was not taking anything to prevent pregnancy. Her parents never discussed the consequences of having sex; rather, they obscured them. They made sure she was clothed, fed, and made good grades in school. To Shawny, her parents were more like a big brother and sister than a mother and father.

After having sex, Mr. Baldwin climbed into the driver's seat, and Shawny followed him and took her place on the passenger's side.

"Where would you like me to drop you off?" he said as he glanced over, reaching for her breast to assist her with buttoning her blouse.

"Take me around the corner, I'll catch the bus from there." she replied. She ran her fingers up and down his arm as he continued to button her blouse. She really didn't have intentions of catching the bus; she was headed to a family member's house to call one of her guy friends to take her home. When she got there, she noticed a group of people hanging around her aunt's front porch. After speaking and making small talk with everyone she knew, she made her way to the telephone to call her friend to pick her up.

Shawny knew it would take a while before the person she paged would call, so she took a seat on the sofa and began to think about Mr. Baldwin. She could clearly picture him leaving his wife for her after she graduated from school. This was only her fantasy; not once had he ever made such a statement to her. She reasoned that he couldn't be happy at home since he managed to sneak away with her from time to time. Gasping at the thought of being with him, she was distracted by someone calling her name. It was the return call she had been waiting for, and after hanging up the telephone she realized she had forgotten to call Co–Co. "I'll just call her when I get home," she sighed as she made her way to the bathroom to freshen up for the friend who was coming to take her home.

When Shawny arrived home, she helped her parents by setting the table for dinner. Sitting down to a family dinner was a systematic routine for Shawny, unlike Co–Co, whose parents were deceased, and Vicki, who had lost both of her parents to the harsh addiction of drugs.

Shawny's parents thought the world of her. Whatever she wanted, they made sure she had. This was their way of showing their appreciation to her for making good grades in school. There were a few things she lacked in life, though. One of them was communication with her parents. They didn't know anything about her unless she told them. They both thought that because she was an A student, and because she didn't have a boyfriend, she was not sexually active. They also didn't bother to spend a lot of quality time as a family; in fact, the only time both of them saw their daughter at the same time was during dinner at night, or breakfast in the morning. Conversations about sex, drugs, and safety were never brought up at all during their family gatherings. They figured she was definitely on the right road to becoming an outstanding young lady with a bright future ahead of her. Although her parents were together and around, at times she felt distant from them because she had learned to do adult things without any instruction or guidance from her parents.

After dinner Shawny made that call to Co–Co. She pretty much had an idea of what the conversation was going to be about. She was hesitant at first about making the call, but then she thought. *Who is she? I can kiss whomever I want to kiss!* After the fourth ring, Co–Co picked up. Shawny asked her if she was sleeping, and she responded. "Nah… I'm just lying here looking at the television. I thought you were going to call me after you were done with your after school program. It's almost ten o'clock, what happened to you?" Co–Co had a lot of bass in her voice. "Why are you messing around with Kevin Barnes? Shawny, you really need to slow down, girl. I was very angry with you today, and I am really not trying to be your mother or anything like that. I just wish you would be more careful about the way you are carrying yourself these days. Don't get me wrong, I'm going to be your friend regardless of what a lot of people have to say about you. But sometimes I do get concerned with my reputation and what is being said about Vicki and me because of your involvement with these dudes from around the way. Why must you be so outspoken all of the time? I've heard a lot of stories lately, and personally, I'm tired of hearing them. Nevertheless, I defend you when I know that half of what I hear is the truth. Listen… all I'm really trying to tell you is to calm it down or cut it out. Males are going to be around forever."

With tears filling her eyes, Shawny held on to the telephone, constantly nodding her head, literally agreeing with everything her concerned friend had to say. Defensively she said, "You are right…yeah, I do have a thing for being around males and yes, I sometimes get a little out of control. But lately you and Vicki have been teaming up without me. So what am I supposed to do, just sit around those fake broads from around the corner? My mother is not hip to anything, and my father could care less about what is going on with me. All they care about is if I am making good grades, and you know yourself that the girls around the way don't like me for real. They are all jealous, and the ones who pretend to like me, they only want to be around me so they can borrow my clothes. So instead of being fake, and being around girls who pretend like it's all about me, I call my male friends. I like the attention. I like when they compliment me, take me out, and make me feel important and good about myself. As far as you and Vicki are concerned... I don't need either one of you. She's always trying to rule everybody with her fake, want–to–be–a–big–baller attitude, and you... with your lil 'I have a future' mess. I don't need y'all, so if you think I am embarrassing to be around, don't be around me!" By that time the tears were pouring down her cheeks and her voice sounded quite shaky.

On the other end of the telephone, Co–Co was outraged. She couldn't believe that Shawny had the nerve to turn the whole situation around to make herself the victim, the one who was misunderstood. This was supposed to have been a reality check to a smart friend, who could do so much better as a person if she didn't think with what was between her legs. Basically she wanted Shawny to know that she didn't owe anything to the guys with whom she hung out. "Yeah… you know what? You are right, Shawny. Maybe we don't need to be around each other anymore, because, yep…I do have a future, and being around people who think I don't is not smart for me at all. Girl, you are blessed, you have both of your parents to support you, and when things get hectic they are there for you. Me, I have an old, sixty something–year–old man who can't afford to hear another disappointment in his life. Everybody keeps saying stuff like, I hope Shawny doesn't turn out bad or negative hanging around Vicki and Co–Co. Huh, little do they know, because you are the worst of the three of us, and you have a mother and a father at home."

Shawny started to interrupt Co–Co, but Co–Co's voice got louder and that silenced Shawny.

"Hold on, let me finish, Shawny. I let you talk; now it's your turn to listen to me. You would think that I would be the one out there looking for affection, seeing how I'm losing something or someone all of the time. But no, I just keep going. I make it happen because I don't want to be a failure. Now Vicki... yeah, she sells drugs, but you and I both know she goes to school every day and she takes care of herself. She has major problems besides being out there throwing bricks, but nevertheless you don't hear or see her out here freaking and acting like a young hoochie momma because her parents don't pay attention to her, do you? So don't throw that attention mess out there. As a matter of fact, I talk to Vicki the same way about her safety and hustling as I am talking to you. If you don't want to hang with us anymore, that's fine with me. I won't call you and don't call me. Personally, your lil mommy and daddy problems, not to mention your 'I need attention' problem couldn't touch my 'I must prove them all wrong' problem." Without hesitation, Co–Co slammed down her telephone, hanging up loudly in Shawny's ear. Then she shouted, "Big Dummy!"

The next morning Vicki arrived earlier than usual and before she could reach the top of the stairs, she heard the sound of Co–Co's door unlocking. When Co–Co opened her door she was surprised to see Vicki standing there. When they got into the car, Co–Co began filling Vicki in on the telephone conversation she and Shawny had had the night before. Their conversation lasted all the way to school. By the time Vicki had settled into a parking space, they had seen Shawny ride past in a convertible BMW with another new male friend.

Vicki and Co–Co both sat there, and as the car drove by Shawny glanced at both of them with a smirk on her face. She gracefully turned her head as if she owned the world.

"Look at your girl," Co–Co said to Vicki as she nudged her head in Shawny's direction. Showing no expression, Vicki threw her backpack across her shoulder and made her way through the school building's double doors. She didn't want to get involved. She knew it was impossible for Co–Co to reach Shawny. She also knew that something was going to happen to her if she kept jumping in and out of cars with different guys. Although she was humble and mature about handling chaos among the three of them, Vicki couldn't help feeling a little angry about what Shawny had to say about her. Instead of confronting her, she thought it would be in Shawny's best interest to keep her distance.

The bell rang, signaling the students that the first period of class was ending. As the students filled the hallways, Shawny spotted Vicki. The tension between the two girls was so thick a chainsaw couldn't cut it. Shawny pretty much figured that Co–Co would tell Vicki about their conversation, which would cause Vicki to have an attitude with her. She was kind of surprised to only get a long stare. She thought it was going to lead into an argument. Then she thought to herself that maybe Co–Co hadn't told Vicki what she had to say about her being a fake baller after all. In her mind, she thought that maybe Vicki was mad at her because Co–Co was mad at her. Either way she didn't really care, she was not going to break or bow down to either one of them. She continued on her way to class, and so did Vicki.

During the final class of the day, an announcement was made for all of the seniors to report to the auditorium to have their measurements taken for their caps and gowns. This meant Shawny would have to face both of them again that afternoon. By the time the seniors filled the auditorium, Shawny didn't see what she now called her new "playa haters." It was hard to find anybody. She assumed they were not coming or that they had already given their measurements and had left the building.

Shawny decided to take a seat and wait for the line to shorten. She sat close to the front, where the teachers were organizing papers and issuing invitations. When she glanced to her left she spotted

Co–Co standing next to Mr. Baldwin, assisting him with the measurement of the caps. At first she wanted to approach her, but she reconsidered. With anger in her eyes, Shawny walked toward both of them to have her measurements taken. Mr. Baldwin treated her no differently than any of the other students. When he took her measurements, he yelled them out to Co–Co, and then she confirmed them, wrote them down, and issued Shawny her invitations. They both moved on to the next student.

Co–Co heard an annoyed, huffing sound as the aggravated Shawny went storming by. Co–Co knew she was getting to Shawny, and she didn't waste any time paying her any attention, either. In fact, she was kind of glad to see her move through the line in such a quick manner, because there were a lot of seniors waiting to be fitted for their caps and gowns. Time went by and many students needed to have their information recorded. Unfortunately it was getting late, and Mr. Baldwin and Co–Co were becoming restless, so they made an announcement that the sizing would continue the following day after class.

Co–Co was relieved and went skipping her way up the aisle. She went racing through the hall, hoping to find Vicki. When she stepped outside, she spotted Vicki's car but noticed that Vicki had not yet made her way out of the building, so she decided to wait for her by the car. While sitting on Vicki's car, Co–Co noticed a note placed under the windshield wiper. She assumed the note had been written by Shawny and that she had finally realized that the two of them were the only real friends she had, they would be the only ones to take up for her when people talked trash about her. Co–Co figured the note was a letter of apology or it was a secret crush letter for Vicki. She was wrong—it wasn't from Shawny at all. The note was a letter in reference to an amount of money, a meeting place, and a list of telephone numbers where the person could be reached. She placed the piece of paper back where she found it. She felt kind of nervous and shaky about seeing that note, because thoughts about her past began to haunt her. She remembered seeing similar notes around her uncle and cousins' cars a few times, not to mention the codes and special messages that were displayed on her family member's pagers. Quite naturally it dawned on her that every last one of them was dead or in jail, doing time for selling drugs. Without hesitating she snatched the note and started ripping it to pieces. She knew she had done the right thing and it didn't matter to her that Vicki was going to be angry with her. What mattered was knowing Vicki lived a safe and jail–free life, then she could experience the joy of walking across the stage to receive her diploma with Co–Co and everybody else would be there to congratulate them and cheer them on. That was what she wanted to capture in her mind, not the bad memories of the constant tragic episodes in her family's drama. She didn't want to be the one to accept Vicki's diploma on her behalf because she was unable to make her way across the stage herself.

"Hey…what are you doing?" A voice shouted. Caught off guard, Co–Co quickly opened her closed hand and released the shredded note through her fingers.

"I've been waiting out here for you, that's what I'm doing," Co–Co said as she began reaching to remove her backpack from her shoulders. Throwing the car keys to Co–Co, Vicki made her way to the back of the car to chat with someone who was sitting in a black SUV. Co–Co proceeded to open the car door and settled into the car while Vicki mingled a little.

About five minutes later, Vicki returned to the car, talking on a cellular phone that she had borrowed from the person in the truck. She began pacing around the car during her conversation. She repeatedly asked the person to whom she was talking where they had put it. She didn't have any luck finding the paper, so she headed back toward her friends in the truck. Right away Co–Co knew exactly what Vicki was looking for. She began to get a little edgy, and she decided not to tell Vicki that she had torn up the note. Becoming impatient, she honked the horn and shouted for Vicki to come back to the car.

"Why are you in a hurry? School is out for today, and by the way, we are seniors. It's all about getting that piece of paper on graduation day. The hard part is over. We don't even have homework anymore, and you are putting the press on me to come on."

Adjusting her seatbelt, Vicki asked Co–Co if she had heard any rumors about Shawny being involved with one of the schoolteachers. Apparently during a conversation with the people in the truck, she heard that Shawny was doing a lot of things which she and Co–Co had not known about.

Co–Co responded by telling her no, but she wouldn't put it past her to screw around with one of the teachers. They laughed, then dropped the subject of Shawny and struck up another conversation about school.

"I've made up my mind about where I would like to attend college, Vick, what about you? Are you going to choose soon or what?"

Vicki insisted that they change the subject. "Co–Co, don't start talking about colleges again. We haven't had a chance to enjoy being out of school yet and you're already discussing colleges? I know you are striving to make your grandfather proud of you, but Renée, I am just not thinking about college right now. I don't know… I guess I don't feel the same way about attending college after we graduate as you do." Vicki told Co–Co that she might or might not go off to college. She went on to say that at least she could feel proud about graduating high school with a high grade point average. Although she sounded sincere, she couldn't get over her jealousy; at the time she had too much pride to tell Co–Co that she too wanted a scholarship. After going back and forth about how they felt about school, Vicki asked Co–Co if she wanted to keep her car until she came back from putting in some work around the way.

Co–Co said no in a very sarcastic way, andthen demanded that Vicki take her home. "You know I don't have a license, and I'm not going to wait around Valley Avenue until you are through doing whatever it is that you do around there, so nope… take me home."

With a crooked grin on her face, Vicki shook her head in disbelief. "Okay. Man… are you sure that you're a Jackson child? I mean, I know you can fight, I know you know how to dress well. You look like a Jackson, you sound like a Jackson, but sometimes, Black, you act like a lil Vanessa Huckstable from the *Cosby Show*."

Co–Co laughed along with Vicki. She had certainly made it clear to Vicki that she honestly loved her family to death, and that she would never forget where she came from. She just didn't want to carry on the negative action of having people respect her because she came from a popular family who lived in the 'hood. Soon the conversation began to get serious again. "I just don't want to carry on settling for the things they settled for in their lives. For instance, you... I felt kind of bad to hear you say you don't want to go to college now."

Before Vicki could say another word, Co–Co raised her hand and spoke louder, which caused Vicki's voice to fade away. "You know yourself that people talked bad about us for a while, until they saw we were all about going to school and not just dressing nice every day. Remember, they were saying stuff like 'Vicki and Gary's lil niece are going to drop out and start hustling and freaking just like all the rest of these 'hood-rats and trick-broads around here.' They even said we were a bad influence on Shawny because she was such a good girl, right?"

Co–Co went on and on complimenting Vicki and telling her how proud she was. "Although they talked bad about both of us, we managed to hang in there, Vicki. I hate what I did as far as cutting Shawny off, but she made my decision very easy. I need to be around people who have a desire to achieve, and who will constantly motivate and encourage me to do well. I'm hoping that you open your eyes and see what I see. I'm not knocking the way you handle yourself out here on the block, but I wish you had another way to survive or at least a smarter way of handling your business without having to sling that mess out here in these stupid streets Vicki." Fanning her hand toward her eyes to prevent her tears from falling, she reached for the door.

"C'mon, Black, don't cry. I didn't know you were feeling this strongly about me going to school. I can't promise you I will go, but I will check out a few, and if I change my mind, you will be the very first to know, all right?" Vicki's pager began to sound off non–stop, distracting the girls from finishing their conversation about their futures and exactly what Vicki must do if she decided to simply graduate and get a regular 9–to–5 job.

The girls arrived at Co–Co's house and Co–Co began to get out of the car, but before closing the car door she leaned in toward Vicki and advised her to be careful. As she headed in the direction of her building she spotted her aunt leaving one of the apartment units, and it didn't take long for her aunt to notice that Co–Co had seen her exiting a crack house, where drug users bought crack and sold any and everything to get high, some females even prostituted themselves to make money so they could purchase crack to get high. She knew her aunt wasn't one of the users who chose to sell goods from her house, and that was for certain.

"Hey Renée, how is my gorgeous niece doing? Look at you, girl, looking just like your momma!"

Co–Co didn't say a word. She just stood there with a pleasant smile, blushing a little. She knew her aunt was just making small talk, trying to pretend as if she hadn't just copped some crack from inside the apartment unit. After talking nonsense for a few minutes, Co–Co decided she would leave. She saw that her aunt was acting very edgy and jittery, which basically meant that she was ready to "beam up, Scotty", smoke the crack. Co–Co told her aunt she would see her later, and her aunt headed down toward the basement, where she was going before she saw Co–Co watching her. It wasn't a surprise to Co–Co. She was very aware of what her tweaked–out aunt was doing, and without any concern, she made her way upstairs to her apartment unit.

About twenty minutes later, Co–Co's aunt knocked at her door. When Co–Co went to the peephole to see who was knocking, she saw her aunt standing outside. Co–Co ignored her for a few minutes, but when the knocks became louder, she got very annoyed and decided to open the door just enough to stick her head out into the hallway, to ask her nervous aunt why she was banging on the door like a madwoman and exactly what it was she wanted.

"I have to use the bathroom. Can I come in?" Co–Co answered her with a high-pitched voice. "No, go back downstairs to use the bathroom! You know that Granddaddy told you that you couldn't come in here when he is not home. I knew you were going to try to pull that stuff on me. No!" Co–Co went on and on about the things her aunt had done to end up in that position. Co–Co felt bad about showing tough love to her aunt and she really wanted to let her in, but she couldn't disobey her grandfather, so her decision was final. After pleading to come in for about what seemed like twenty-five minutes, her aunt finally gave up and headed down the stairwell. Co–Co shut the door and watched her pitiful aunt fade away through the peephole, and although she felt sorry for her, she knew she had made the best choice. After she watched her disappear, she turned around, shut her eyes tightly, and gently pounded her head on the door. She couldn't help feeling bad about turning her aunt away. She knew how bad her aunt was addicted to drugs, and regardless of how much tough love was shown, nothing could change the fact that her aunt had a problem. She just wasn't going to give her another opportunity to steal from her or her grandfather again.

On the other side of town Vicki was getting her hustle on. She was serving weight packages constantly, and the money was coming to her so quickly that she was unconcerned about collecting debts from previous clients whom she had dealt with before she received the packages from Co–Co. It seemed a little unreal to her because she had called the bigwigs in the beginning, but now she was rolling just like the bigwigs, and people were calling *her* for work now. She broke down both packages to sell soft, powdered cocaine as well as hard, crack cocaine. Her pager was blowing up but she was very attentive when it came to responding to each and every person who had paged her. *So far, so good,* she thought. Everything was going swell for her; she had school in order, her grades were on point and above average, her gear was tight, everybody liked and showed respect to her in the 'hoods throughout the district, and most of all, she was completely out of debt. She didn't owe anyone anything, and that was the best part of it all, she had her own stuff out there on the block. It wasn't a secret; everybody knew she was dealing and she really didn't care. Most of the people were a bit jealous, but the majority of the neighborhood respected her and looked out for her when the jump–outs (the police) were coming through.

In most areas of her life she was known for being humble and the jokester of the three girls, but when trouble came her way, she made it known that she wasn't a weakling. Vicki had the strength of a grown man and could drop a girl like a bad habit, if she had to defend herself. The only time she had to get tough was when some of her female clients would show disrespect by paying her in increments or owing her for months; other than those obvious conflicts she kept a cool head. To her, selling drugs was just like having a job. She totally understood how Co–Co felt about the things she was out there doing to survive, but on the other hand, she believed that having money in her pocket wasn't a bad thing either.

That night, Vicki sold all of her packages, and decided to leave the block a little earlier than usual. She always parked her car two or three blocks away from where she dealt her drugs, because if her clients owed her money they would avoid the area if they thought she was around. The other reason was if she needed to stash her packages, her car was safer than using one of the crack houses around the way. This was her daily routine, and a smart way to handle her business, so she thought. She had a systematic plan; she would park on Ninth Street, walk down to Seventh Street, and serve those who wanted weight on Seventh and Eighth Streets. This meant that by the time she returned to Ninth Street where her car was parked, all she had to do was drive off the block and when necessary, repeat her tactics in other neighborhoods throughout the district. She returned to her car with a few requests for more packages and a pocket full of money, and besides laughing and talking trash to a few people from around Ninth Street, there seem to be nothing else for her to do, except get in her car and leave for home.

While walking toward her car her pager began to sound off, she ignored it because she had her mind made up. Her plans were to go home, wash her clothes, cook something to eat, and watch a little television.

When she got to her car she headed toward the trunk to change a few of her CD's around, and as she made her way to the driver's side of the car, she heard her name being called. "Hey, Vicki! Vicki!" The voice shouted her name about three more times, trying to get her attention.

Although she looked around to see who was calling her, she continued to get into the car. She glanced over her shoulder and did not see anyone, so she looked across the street once again. Instead of staying halfway into the car, she got inside and closed the car door. As soon as she cranked the car, a short, unfamiliar, light–skinned boy appeared in front of her car, huffing and panting for air as if he was out of breath. He tapped on the driver's side window to get her attention.

With a look of curiosity upon her face, Vicki rolled down her window a little, just enough to hear what the boy had to say. "Hey... you are Vicki, right?"

Without hesitating, Vicki answered. "Yeah, what's up?" She didn't feel like she was in danger because she was in her zone, plus, she figured that if any problems arose with the young guy, she could easily get help from somebody around the way.

Unfortunately, the streets were quiet except for a few crack–heads, which only appeared when they roamed from building to building.

Anxiously, he asked her again, "You're Vicki right? My man told me to holla at you if I wanted some soft, do you got dat?"

Vicki was not familiar with this boy at all. "Your man? Who is your man?" she asked as she adjusted the volume on her car stereo.

Before he could give her an answer, the boy pulled out a gun and demanded that she open the door. "Don't try to be slick, 'cause if you try to pull off, I will bust off on you before you are able to shift into gear. Unlock the door and get in the passenger seat."

Frantically, she eased her way across to settle into the passenger seat. Before he had made the threat to shoot her, she had thought about pressing the car horn to attract attention to her car, but then she didn't because she knew no one would pay the horn any attention. It would have only made her situation worse, and besides, she knew that to many people an actual robbery probably would have looked like Vicki decided to let one of her friends drive her car. This was turning into a nightmare for her—to be robbed by someone she had never seen before in a neighborhood where she was comfortable and well known, but quite helpless because the streets were empty. Then out of nowhere came another young guy. He hopped into the back seat and instructed the driver to pull off.

Vicki was trembling with fear but not once did she let her feelings show. She just sat there hoping that the two boys would only take her money—not her life. When the passenger in the back seat asked the driver to pull into the alley, Vicki immediately became aggressive. She turned toward the driver, told him how much money she had in her pockets, and insisted that they let her go. "Please don't kill me! I have about four or five thousand dollars on me and y'all can have it all. Take my car, take my jewelry, take my money, just please, don't take my life!" She cried to the two thugs, and as the tears fell profusely from her eyes, she heard, as if for the first time, all of the things her brother and

Co–Co had been saying. She pictured their faces and heard their voices as they spoke loudly and clearly to her about giving up her street life. She remembered the conversation in front of Co–Co's apartment building when her friend expressed her concerns about Vicki's throwing stones out there in the streets. She thought back to how her brother had shaken his finger in her face and told her to slow down and get out of the game before she got both of them in a lot of trouble, and to do it before it was too late.

This time it was certainly too late. She even thought about the times her colleagues had been involved in tragic robberies, and the worst thing that had happened to them was they got shot and lived to tell about it. She was at the point where she wished the boys would shoot her in an arm or a leg, take the money and the car, and let her live. This was a very stupid way of thinking, but at the time it made a lot of sense to her. Besides, in her situation she really had only those two choices. If she lived, she thought this robbery would be an enormous wake–up call for her, because she had been feeling a false sense of safety in the neighborhood the entire time she had been slinging.

When the passenger lounging in the back seat demanded that the driver pull into the alley again, Vicki frantically said "No! Let me out... y'all are going to try to rape me. Let me go!" Although her heart was beginning to race with fear, she was certain that if these two boys raped her, they were definitely going to have to kill her, because she was going to put up a fight.

The second she began to yell, the guy in the back seat clicked his gun and aimed it at her head. "Shut up. Ain't nobody gonna rape you, slim, you got my game twisted, Shorty! I don't have to take booty from no broad. I'm on money, and if you ever part you lips with that word 'rape' again up in here, I swear on everything that I love, I'll blast your head up off your shoulders, girl. What's wrong wit you?"

Vicki just sat there weeping and shaking as if she were a leaf on a tree. When they pulled into the alley, the backseat passenger got out of the car and pulled out a pocketknife. He began stabbing her tires when all of a sudden the driver fired his gun. He shot Vicki in the head. Blood was everywhere.

"What are you doing man? I told you to pistol–whip her and to take her rings and stuff, I didn't say blast the broad. What's wrong wit you? We didn't even ask her where everything was, stupid. How are we gonna get the rest of the stuff? She's dead now!"

His plans had been to flatten all four tires and torture her a little until she confessed where her stash was hidden. He had not planned to kill or shoot her; however, the driver had. He knew she knew his face, and although Vicki hadn't admitted to seeing him before, he knew that if she saw him again she would easily identify him, and that would lead to more drama later on.

"Man… she knew who I was, she was crying and saying, 'Herb don't kill me'. I never told her who I was, and you didn't mention my name once. I think she remembered my face because she saw me with tall Rodney and Eli a long time ago, so I just busted off on her 'cause I don't want beef with them dudes from around Linda Pollin over this broad, do you?"

They both started reaching in her pockets and scrambling through her car, searching for money and whatever else they thought was valuable. After they got all of the goods, they both fled the scene, and one of the boys took Vicki's keys with him.

It wasn't long before the police were knocking on Vicki's door to deliver the bad news to her brother, K.C. It seemed that someone from the area where the shooting took place called the police because they saw two teenage boys vandalizing a car in back of an alley. But it wasn't until the body was found that they knew why the gunshots were fired. They thought the boys were just goofing off.

Vicki had been shot and tortured like an animal, one detective said, and she was pronounced dead on the scene. Apparently before the two guys left, they had finished what they had started by shooting her four times more, and then they repeatedly stuck a knife into her face, neck, and breast area. When the coroners took her away, her body left a trail of blood from the car to the meat wagon. One of the sick, demented

105

thugs had decided to shoot her in her private area. That was his way of retaliating for the insulting "rapist" comment.

The next morning Co–Co was awakened by the sound of her telephone. Before answering, she always screened her calls by looking at her caller ID box. First, she looked at her clock. The time displayed was 6:30 a.m. She got out of bed to look at the box. "Shawny," she whispered. Immediately she jumped back into her bed and pulled the covers over her head. The telephone rang about five or six times before her voice mail picked up. For about a minute or two her telephone was silent, and then the ringing began once again. Angrily, Co–Co answered, "What…what do you want girl!" Shawny was crying so loudly that Co–Co could barely understand her. She asked her to slow down, and then asked her who got killed last night. Shawny repeated herself, only this time she made sure Co–Co heard her, because all she kept saying was, "She's gone, Vicki is gone—they killed her—she's gone."

In disbelief, Co–Co fell to the floor and mumbled, "Who told you this? Where did you hear this? If something had happened to Vicki, K.C. would have called me by now. I think somebody—"

Before she could complete her sentence, she was interrupted by another call. She told Shawny to hold while she answered the other line. It was K.C. He was calling with the same news. Of course she didn't take it too well—she shouted and screamed "no", and repeated the word "no" continuously until she began crying. As she cried, she told K.C. to stop telling her that Vicki was dead. "Stop it! Don't say that. Tell me she's been hurt, but please, do not tell me that she is gone, because I won't believe you—I just can't—what happened?" Co–Co was so upset she couldn't think straight. Words were, as they say, "coming out the side of her neck".

"Oh my goodness, she is not going to graduate with me."

It was hard for K.C. to calm Co–Co down over the telephone; in fact, her sadness began to rub off on him. Co–Co felt helpless because no one was there to comfort her at the time, but she managed to straighten up a little for the sake of K.C., who she knew felt much worse because Vicki was his sister. She eventually got herself together and rushed over to their house to be with him.

Shawny figured that the other line would be a call in reference to the death of their friend, so instead of holding on the telephone, waiting for Co–Co to click back over, she decided to make her way to K.C.'s house so she could be with Co–Co. She knew Co–Co would be going there as soon as possible. By the time Co–Co arrived, K.C.'s house was filled with people. Many of their family members and neighborhood friends came over to support him during his tragic loss.

As usual during sympathy gatherings, the elder women were there to hug and comfort K.C. and Vicki's peers, as well as each other. Everyone was aware of the life that Vicki had lived, yet it was very hard for them to understand how someone could commit such a horrible crime against such an outstanding young person who had such potential. She wanted to do better and clean up her lifestyle, but she sometimes had problems figuring out the difference between the right and wrong ways to handle certain issues in her life. By the time Vicki's story aired on the local news station, her family members were angry, but not surprised with the way the media told the story. They made her out to be an undercover outcast who used high school as a front to deal her drugs. Not once did they mention that she was an honor roll student or that she occasionally volunteered her time to help the homeless and those less fortunate than her. After discussing how mad and disappointed they all were with the lies told by the media, Co–Co sat on the edge of the couch feeling responsible for Vicki's death. She thought silently to herself, *none of this would have happened if I would have just flushed all that stuff down the toilet. This is all my fault.* She blamed herself and felt really guilty about participating in that drug transaction with Vicki and her acquaintances.

Teary–eyed and her heart filled with guilt, Co–Co made her way through the living room area to answer the front door. The person's knock was quite similar to that of an officer of the law, but it was

Shawny. Immediately the two girls grabbed each other and held each other very tightly. After the girls had given each other a pat on the back, Shawny pulled away and asked Co-Co if she was going to be okay. "No!" she shouted, "My best friend is dead. I'm scared, Shawny. I don't know what to do and I can't believe this has happened to her—I just don't believe it!"

Tears began falling from her eyes, and the two girls embraced as sounds of sadness leaked through their mouths. Vicki's brother made his way over to the girls to console them. "Hey c'mon, Ms. Co–Co. You know you are supposed to be the strong one, and you can't keep crying and getting yourself all upset now. We need you, and I know it hurts baby, but you and I both kept telling Victoria that she needed to slow down." He sat down beside both of the girls and assured them that they were going to be all right. "We lost our sister but her spirit will be with us forever, she is going to live forever in our hearts."

It wasn't long before the girls realized that crying and feeling sorry about losing Vicki would not bring her back to life, so they eventually calmed themselves down and began chatting about how funny she was. They went back and forth, telling stories about her different situations with crack–heads around the way. The three of them had a good time going through recent and old pictures of their loved one. Although they were feeling a lot better, guilty thoughts about giving Vicki those packages were constantly on Co–Co's mind. Part of her wanted to tell someone what made Vicki chase that street money the way she did, but the other part of her conscience wished she didn't feel so guilty, because she also thought that whether she had given it to her or not, eventually something bad was going to happen anyway. Co–Co thought hard about what she should do and decided to make K.C. her first concern. She also hoped that if she could ever bring herself to tell him anything, he would understand and not be angry with her.

Besides the many people, the room was full with sympathy cards and flowers. Their Aunt Lynn, the one who had given K.C. the permission to raise Vicki, was quite silent, and remained that way during the entire conversation between her nephew and the girls.

As they transformed their tears into innocent laughter while viewing photos of Vicki, K.C. noticed that his Aunt Lynn was very silent. He couldn't quite decide what the smile on her face meant, so he slid over in her direction with a questioning look upon his face. Before he could ask her why she was smiling so funny, her husky, brisk voice cut him off. "Take those down, K.C. My baby didn't like flowers; she always said that fresh flowers smelled like feet. Y'all running around here feeling sad and crying and everything like my baby is gone…well, she's not, she's right here." She pointed to her heart and smiled. "So please get those flowers out of here and put on some of that noise that my baby liked that used to drive me crazy."

K.C. unlocked his arms from around his aunt's neck and sprang away to get one of Vicki's go–go tapes. "If Ms. Vicki was here she would probably kill me right now, because that girl couldn't stand me messing with her go–go tapes, especially the tapes that Kwame made for her ears only."

Co–Co and Shawny laughed as they agreed with him. "Yep, K.C., that is true, if Vic was here she would have given you that evil look. That girl did not play when it came to her tapes, especially the ones when Donnell and his group were saying…'Hang in there, Miss Vicki, we see you over there, aw… Miss Money–Honey!' Co–Co imitated the lead singer of the band by placing her hand in front of her mouth and speaking through her slightly opened fist. Everybody enjoyed her impressions and the sour feeling of losing Vicki wasn't as bad with a little laughter in the room, at least during Co–Co's little show for her family that evening. While the music played, she made her way toward the area where Shawny was sitting. Shawny was slumped over with her arms crossed on top of her knees, and she nestled her head through the opening of her arms as if she was asleep.

"Are you all right Shawny?"

"Yeah… I'm cool, but I know that you are not," Shawny replied. She was worried about Co–Co distancing herself from her after their friend's funeral service was over. She wanted to apologize for not

113

being a good friend. She had seen how close Co–Co and Vicki were, and she had always felt she was the odd ball of the crew since she had moved out of the hood. So when she felt the need, she decided to play that role since that's what most of her peers thought of her anyway. Feeling out of place as a member of the three girls, she told Co–Co that although she and Vicki hadn't been that close, she had a lot of love for her. She went on to say, "Sometimes I look at my life and wish I could take back a lot of things I have done in my past." For some reason she felt guilty and embarrassed about defending her dumb, promiscuous actions.

Shawny went on and on, apologizing and making excuses for herself, until Co–Co was so confused about what she was getting at, she finally asked Shawny. "What... why are you so sorry? What are you talking about, what's going on?"

Co–Co wasn't prepared for what Shawny had to say next. She was thinking that maybe Shawny was so afraid of death that she wanted to get herself right with God, and that she would start being more responsible for her actions and how she handled herself around males.

Shamefully Shawny whispered, "I think I'm pregnant." Shawny looked away, and then shifted her irritated, red eyes in Co–Co's direction. When she felt Co–Co's eyes shifting her way she immediately looked away, because she was used to Co–Co giving her those disgusted facial expressions. She just couldn't bear to look in her eyes after she told her what was bothering her. It shocked her when Co–Co reached out to hug and comfort her, and assure her that she would be all right. "It's okay. You will have your parents there to help you out if you are pregnant, and you know you can depend on me to help you, right?"

Co–Co's next question got the tears flowing from Shawny's young eyes, and the only answer she could give was the one that Co–Co had expected. "Who is the father, Shawny?"

"I don't know, and I'm afraid to tell any of the people I've slept with, because I'm just not sure." She had unprotected sex with all of her partners, including the young teacher.

Normally, Co–Co would have given her a reality check speech, not to mention a "you should be ashamed of yourself" speech, but not this time. It really wasn't the time or the place to judge Shawny, so Co–Co showed her support and made her feel comfortable about the entire situation. Patting her on the back, Co–Co told her that no matter what happened after she heard the pregnancy test results, she would remain her friend, because she had realized that life was too short to go around being angry about the way she had chosen to live her life. Of course, Co–Co made her promise that they would finish their conversation about why she did not know who the father of her unborn child was.

After talking they headed toward the back room, where most of Vicki's cousins and a few of her good friends were socializing. They hung out in the back room for a while, until they were called to come and join K.C. and his Aunt Lynn in prayer. Co–Co, along with everybody else in the house, was shocked to see Vicki's parents sitting in the room. They were shocked because the father was high and kept nodding' off. They felt sorry for K.C. because just like Co–Co's aunt, his parents were hard–core addicts who did not have permission to enter their family member's homes without supervision.

Seeing him that way reminded Co–Co of a time when Vicki had handed her mother a glass of water for her father through the door because she didn't want them in their apartment. Co–Co felt badly for them, because she knew that if Vicki hadn't been murdered, her parents would've never made it past the door seal of the apartment. After greeting Vicki's mom with a hug, Co–Co took a seat on the couch next to Vicki's father.

"Hey, Renée, how are you holding up, baby? Are you all right?"

"Nah... John, I'm not all right. I feel like they killed a part of me, too." She was very uncomfortable and tried her best to maintain her composure while sitting between Vicki's parents. They both looked and smelled really bad, but none of that mattered to her at the time. Although both of them were high and had been drinking alcohol heavily, their appearance couldn't compare to the feeling of having to bury their young teenage daughter. It was disgusting to glance over into the eyes of Vicki's father. He was as high as a kite. Everybody in the house knew about his unacceptable condition, but no one said anything about him or to him out of respect for Vicki's brother, K.C.

Slowly Co–Co's urge to confront him about his presence built, and she was concerned, yet very blunt, in her approach. With fire in her eyes she stood in front of him and asked, "How can you sit there and disrespect Vicki and K.C. like that, John?"

With a peevish expression, he raised his head slowly and replied, "What, I'm what—girl you don't know what you are talking about. My baby is gone. I'm celebrating 'cause she's in a better place now." He went on to explain why he was intoxicated by saying, "So what? I had a few drinks. I'm still hurting on the inside. Maybe you should pour yourself a few shots of rem–dog—Remy Martin—so that you can lighten up a little bit, Youngn'. You know what I'm sayin'?" Everyone knew he had had a lot more than just a few drinks—he was high and hanging off the edge of the couch toward the floor, headfirst. After his senseless outburst, silence filled the room, and for the rest of the day K.C. simply pretended he did not exist.

After the drama between Vicki's father and Co–Co, their close friends and family members became very agitated with him and prepared to leave so the immediate family could grieve the death of Vicki alone. It took a while, but finally all of the guests had left; everyone, except Shawny and Co–Co. They had gotten permission to stay the night because they wanted to help K.C. and his Aunt Lynn with the funeral arrangements.

Late that evening Vicki's father upset the entire family again. Apparently he had assumed that Vicki had some drugs hidden around the apartment. He had enough nerve to ask K.C. if he knew where they were hidden.

K.C. didn't waste any time. He had had enough of his outrageous outbursts and he became convinced that his father was definitely not worried about the death of his teenage daughter at all. He was more concerned with finding out if his daughter had extras stashed away, so he could get even higher than he already was.

Hurt and very angry, K.C. wasted no time throwing him out. "Get the hell out of my house, John. You have to be the lowest piece of scum living on this earth. I hate you so much right now! How could you stand here asking for drugs? Who do you think you are fooling, huh? Go, you sick bastard, get out of here!" K.C. became very angry—he threw things and shouted from the top of his lungs until his father was out the door. He then turned to his mother and said, "You...I blame you for everything that has happened to us over the years. Are you here plotting to get high too, huh? Are you? 'Cause if you are, guess what? You won't be getting high today, Mother!"

K.C.'s mother stood and with a calm, soft voice she answered his question. "No, and I'm sorry for not being involved in you and your sister's lives. Kevin, you are hurting and I understand that, but I think you are way out of line. Baby, I know that the pain is there, and I will take full responsibility for being a no–good mother, but that man really is hurting, and I'm hurting too. Losing my baby has torn an enormous hole in my heart. I can't change the past and I can't make you forgive me either, but Kevin, I am tired and I can't continue to use drugs and live my life this way. I know it is hard to believe me when I tell you that I'm sorry, and Kevin, I do care."

What started out as an argument simmered down into a sauce of held–back tears. She grabbed her son and held him in her arms for a long time. K.C. cried like a baby and repeated over and over that he forgave her, but he insisted that she had to change. He went on to say that he needed her to be a part of his life, and she agreed. It was beautiful that they were reunited after so many years of neglect, but on the other hand, it was quite shameful that it took the death of her daughter to open his mother's eyes. Both Co–Co and Shawny were there to witness this very emotional conversation. They were both familiar with the family background, and were shocked to see K.C. put his arms around his mom that way. After pulling themselves together, K.C., his mom, and his Aunt Lynn gathered the telephone numbers of the rest of their family and friends to inform them of their loss. Time went by very quickly and it was getting dark, so they all decided to eat dinner and turn in early so they could continue handling things the next morning.

The next morning Co–Co felt a lot better, and was determined to face her last two weeks of school without the presence of her dear friend Vicki. She knew it was going to be hard but she wasn't about to give up. She had to be strong because she felt she was going to walk across that stage for both of them. After getting dressed she sat around waiting for Shawny and K.C. She decided to call her grandfather before heading off to school. After hanging up the telephone, she smiled, she was so happy to hear from the coolest man on the block. She really appreciated him for allowing her to stay over to comfort her friend's family on a school night. When K.C. arrived to drop the girls off for school, all three of them noticed everyone staring and pointing in their direction, as if they were a couple of famous movie stars. K.C. felt a little angry and very uncomfortable as he sat there waiting and watching the girls gather their backpacks. He knew they were hanging around waiting for the girls, so he sarcastically said out loud, "See y'all later. I'm sure all of those fake Washington Post editors over there are waiting for y'all to answer their stupid little questions!"

Co–Co didn't respond. She shut the car door and followed Shawny, who had already ignored two or three students before entering the school building. Before going to homeroom, Co–Co wanted to ask one of the secretaries in the principal's office if she could make an announcement in memory of her best friend, Victoria Carter.

Of course, the answer was yes, but she would have to wait until the second bell for homeroom sounded. The bell rang and she took a deep breath, stepped up to the intercom, and said calmly, "Good morning. My name is Renée Jackson and I would like to share something with my fellow students. The night before last I lost my best friend. I felt sad and it hurt me very badly. We had plans to do many things together. The local media made her out to be such a

123

bad person, but we all know that she was nothing like the person they described in the newspaper. She was great and had a good sense of humor. I'm sure she had a spot in the hearts of those who knew her well. This morning I began writing my announcement down on a piece of paper, but as I started to write, I changed my mind because I didn't want to read from a piece of paper when I could easily speak from my heart. Victoria was murdered viciously, but thoughts of her will live forever in my heart and mind. An honor roll student, a funny person who could make the meanest baby laugh, a dreamer who promised she would stop selling drugs soon. Unfortunately soon wasn't soon enough, because getting rid of drugs is what put her to rest. Her life was a hard and confused life to live, yet she made living in her shoes such a wonderful thing to do. I wish I didn't have to make this announcement this morning, and to all of you students out there, with hopes of making it to the age of seventeen, please do not get involved with selling drugs. Besides Victoria there are a lot of you who are out there slinging, and you're thinking that what happened to her won't happen to you. Well, I'm here to tell you all that yes, it can and it will, because she once told me the exact same thing. I thank you for listening and as my friend Vicki would say, 'you betta believe it, it's real out here'."

After Co–Co's announcement, instead of a moment of silence, the principal asked the entire building to give Victoria Marie Carter congratulations and a loud round of applause for being part of the 1999 graduating class, with honors. The roaring lasted for about five minutes. The principal went on to thank Co–Co over the loudspeaker for being brave enough to voice her honest and deep emotions about her fellow students.

Before heading to her homeroom, Co–Co wanted to stop by Vicki's locker. She couldn't believe her eyes—she smiled continuously as she glanced at the photos of Vicki and one of her ex–boyfriends. "Aw, Vicki, let me find out you still had feelings for Chauncey, look at you… posting all his pictures up in your locker." For some reason she had felt the need to go to Vicki's locker. Because the twelfth graders were done with finals, the only reasons they were attending school was to pick up their caps and gowns, to turn in their books, and to participate in the rehearsal for graduation. After rehearsal Co–Co asked Shawny if she would assist her with cleaning out Vicki's locker. When they were done, they made their way to the school's office to call K.C. to pick them up. K.C. arrived, but he wasn't alone—his mom was with him, and she looked stunning. He must have put together one of Vicki's outfits and helped her with her hair because she definitely did not look like the same tore down addict that walked through his door the night before last.

As they loaded the car with all of Vicki's things, they made funny comments about Vicki and her junky locker. It was her mother who cracked the first joke and broke the ice. "Whew-wee... Vicki was always junky, but that locker must have been her second home. She had everything in that thing, I mean everything!" She went on to say that K.C. had been a little junky too when he was younger, and they all laughed and continued to have a good time, thinking about Vicki and all of the wild and crazy things she used to say and do to people.

Shawny was laughing, but inside she was crying because she had a situation that was making her feel terrible. She felt so bad about being irresponsible that at one point she wished she could trade places with Vicki. As she daydreamed and looked out into the city, her daze was broken by a nudge of Co–Co's elbow.

"Hey, Shawny, are you okay?"

She was speechless. All she could do was nod her head yes. Her secret was a false secret—she was not pregnant, she was told to get a second HIV test done, and she didn't want to admit that to Co–Co, so she lied instead and said she thought she might be pregnant.

Time passed and the funeral took place in one of the smallest funeral homes, but one which was well known for putting young people to rest. People from all over came to pay their respects, and although it was a memorial meeting to say goodbye to Vicki, to some it was a chance to mingle and see who was who among the hustlers. The guys from uptown N.W. were checking out all of Vicki's Southside buddies from S.E., and the humble N.E. boys were eyeing those sassy S.W. friends of hers. Even the young guys and girls from Baltimore, Maryland, and Norfolk, Virginia came out to show their respect to the well-known teenager, who had thought with her heart when it came to the people she knew and loved. Everyone was so well–dressed at the funeral. A person could have mistaken Mason's Funeral Home for the Grammy awards, if one hadn't known any better.

Because of the serious gunshot wounds, viewing of Vicki's body was prohibited. The mortician insisted that the family have a closed–casket funeral.

There she was, the daughter of the 'hood, Victoria Marie Carter, a.k.a. "Vicki". K.C. had an enormous picture of her, which displayed her bright, warm smile—in fact it was the cap and gown photo, which was featured in the school's yearbook.

As her friends and family members walked up to touch the casket and to say their last good-byes, it seemed as if the receiving line would not end. The visitors kissed and hugged Vicki's brother, her mom, and their special Aunt Lynn, and they complimented them on what a special teenager she was, and said how nice they had put her away to rest with the Lord.

With all the sorrows filling the air, Shawny forgot all about her situation completely. Her parents were there to support their daughter's loss and to pay their respects to Vicki and her family as well.

Co–Co's grandfather held her hand and spoke to her very softly. He told her to release her feelings and thank God for accepting Vicki into Heaven, and he pointed toward the roof of the building and said, "She's all right now, Renée, she's up there with your mom and dad, your grandma, aunt Ronnail, and your uncle Gary. They will fill her in on how to get her wings. You don't have to be strong all of the time, it's okay to cry. Let it out—it's all right."

Co–Co stared down at the floor with tears flowing from her eyes. She couldn't help but wonder whether Vicki would still be alive if she had not given her those two packages. Her conscience was eating away at her and she wished she had just flushed those two packages down the toilet. When the time came for her to read her poem, she just stood there. "No, no, no...I can't do it!" She let out a loud cry and ran straight for the casket. "I'm sorry, I'm so sorry, Vicki, please get up. C'mon, get up!" This went on for a minute or two. Everyone knew how close the two of them had been, and because of all Co–Co's hardships and the sad times she'd faced when losing family members in the past, those who knew her very well were surprised to see her break down the way she did. They thought she would be as strong and brave as she was during the burials of her own family members.

After the funeral service was over, the repast was held at K.C.'s house. His apartment was flooded with people who stopped by to leave money, cards, food, and anything else they thought would lift Vicki's brother's sprits during his time of grieving.

Since Vicki and Co–Co had been more like sisters than neighborhood friends, K.C. thought it was only right to give her all of Vicki's clothing. "Co–Co, take whatever you want, I'm sure Ms. Vicki wouldn't want anybody else to have her clothes but you. I kept a lot of the shoes, boots, a few handbags, and some slick lil trendy outfits for our mother, but you can have everything else if you want it, okay?"

Co–Co heard every word he said, but she didn't budge at all. She sat on the edge of Vicki's bed until she had whimpered herself to sleep.

Shawny was at the other end of the bed and had already dozed off. She was more than welcome to have some of Vicki things as well, but because she had fallen asleep, K.C. would mention it to her later. Meanwhile K.C. and his mother went into his room to talk about committing to their reunion. The conversation involved what he expected from his mother if they were going to be living together. He wanted his mother to clean up her life, and knew it wasn't going to happen overnight, but he did expect it to happen. "Ma, you can stay in Vicki's room but you have to get clean—I mean *completely* clean. No weed, no Remy, no cigarettes, no nothing. John is not welcome here. He didn't even come to his own daughter's funeral; how sick is that!"

K.C. went on to say how his Aunt Malisa mentioned how out of it his father had been. She told him that his father kept nodding, scratching, and mumbling nonsense about how he didn't want to see his baby girl like that. K.C. didn't excuse his father for his behavior. He told his aunt it was just a cop–out. With tears in his eyes, he turned to his mother and said. "He claimed that he didn't want to remember her like that…whatever!"

For a second, K.C. thought she was going to defend him again as she had done in the past, but not this time. She held her son's hand and assured him that she was through with all of that dumb stuff. "Kevin, I'm tired of living like a bum. I mean it. It's sad to say but I have to admit this. It took the death of my seed; I mean my own daughter's precious life for me to finally wake up. I know that sounds terrible, but it's true. My child had to die in order for me to notice that I have a family who loves me. I had an outstanding pair of children who turned out one thousand percent better than both of their parents. I can't get high anymore—I just can't touch what helped kill my baby. I can't and I won't do it, I promise!" She went near one of Vicki's pictures and held it close to her heart and with her eyes shut, she softly said. "Rest in peace, my sweetie, in Jesus' name I pray. Amen."

Soon it was time for bed. The apartment had cleared out, and everyone who had decided to stay the night with K.C. and his mom decided to turn in for the night.

A couple of days went by, Vicki's mother got dressed and told K.C. that she was going over to the school to pick up Vicki's awards and her diploma.

With a look of amazement in his eyes, K.C. complimented his mother on how well she looked. "Whoa, Ma look at you, you look so cute. Now that's the Momma I want to know and love."

Blushing from ear to ear, she danced her way toward the door and waved her hand back and forth as if she was a contestant in a beauty contest. When she arrived at the school building, the feeling of being a mother for the very first time sent chills through her body. She immediately thought for the first time in

133

twenty-six years, she honestly knew what it felt like to be a responsible parent. After signing in at the security desk, she made her way to the school office to meet with Vicki's principal. Her presence was puzzling to most of the teachers who knew Vicki because they were only familiar with her Aunt Lynn and brother K.C. They had never been introduced to Vicki's mother before, so to see her inquiring about "her daughter's information" was a shock to them all. After being introduced to a few of the school staff members she returned home with nothing but an enormous smile on her face.

Time passed, and graduation day for Co–Co and Shawny drew near. They were both excited about going shopping for graduation clothes and shoes, and by the time they were headed for the third store, Shawny was feeling a little short–winded and very nauseated. Her forehead was covered with tiny beads of sweat, but not once did she bother to tell Co–Co she wasn't feeling well, she just stood there and pretended to show interest as she listened to Co–Co inquire about the clothing in the store. She knew she would eventually go through certain changes after being diagnosed with what doctors called the first stages of an incurable disease.

Shawny's weakness was becoming noticeable to the customers around her, but before she could get the attention of Co–Co, who was holding a conversation with one of the sales associates, she fainted, losing control of her shopping bags and her expensive, tiny clutch purse. She was stretched out in the corner of the department store, and immediately Co–Co rushed to her aid. "Call an ambulance, please...she's pregnant!" she shouted.

Co–Co couldn't believe what had happened to Shawny, because one minute they were laughing and playing around in the mall, and the next thing she knew a person had passed out. When Co–Co finally realized that the person lying on the floor was Shawny, she became nervous and began to panic because she was worried about Shawny's unborn child. When they got to the hospital, Shawny was immediately rushed to the intensive care unit.

Co–Co rushed to the pay phone to contact Shawny's parents, and when her parents arrived they were taken into a family room and were there for what seemed like hours. Co–Co worried and became very impatient because no one was telling her anything about her pregnant friend's condition. "What's going on? Where is Shawny? And how come everybody is being so quiet in that room over there?" she asked the nurse at the front desk as she pointed in the direction of the three doctors and Shawny's parents.

Unable to give Co–Co any answers, the nurse slowly hunched her shoulders as if she was just as puzzled as Co–Co was. Minutes later the door opened and out came the three doctors, Co–Co impatiently made her way across the hall to the room where Shawny's parents were.

Judging by the look on Shawny's mother's face, one could have assumed that the doctors had just given her an outrageous hospital bill. Before Co–Co could speak, Shawny's mother asked her to please leave the room. "Please, Renée, I need time to be alone. I can't believe what those doctors just told me!"

She went on to tell Co–Co that she wasn't being mean, but she suggested that the young girl go home because they definitely were going to be there all night. "I understand that you want to be a friend to my daughter, but this is really crazy. I'll let her know you are here, and thanks so much for calling the people for her, thank you so much." As Shawny's mother stood there with one foot holding the door open, she waved her hand slowly, directing Co–Co to leave the room. Co–Co had known that Shawny's parents wouldn't take her pregnancy news too well, but she hadn't expected her mother to act the way she did either.

During the drive home, Co–Co's grandfather asked if she was excited about graduation. To please him she answered yes, but deep down inside she wanted to say no. Exactly how exciting would it be to walk across the stage two weeks after burying a best friend, not to mention escorting another friend to the emergency room the week before graduating? These were her thoughts and held–back feelings about her grandfather's question; however, she also knew exactly how important it was that he witness and cheer her on as she made her way across the stage to receive her diploma.

It wasn't long before her grandfather began to inquire about what had happened to Shawny. "What was wrong with your little friend today?"

With an honest look upon her face, she gave him half of the truth. "She fainted. I guess she was getting exhausted from running around back and forth, and in and out of all of the different stores as we were shopping, Granddaddy."

Confused and curious, Co–Co's grandfather couldn't figure out how someone Shawny's age could all of a sudden become exhausted by running from store to store shopping. So he asked her to run that story by him again, only this time he wanted her to be more specific, which meant he wanted to know exactly what made her fall out. He was certain that those nice department stores had enough central air to keep both of them very cool during their little shopping spree. "She's pregnant, Granddaddy, and I really think she was starving herself or doing something wrong so that she could miscarry her baby, because her parents didn't know anything."

Her grandfather shook his head in disgust and said, "That's a dag–on shame. Shame on her. How could she do a stupid thing like that? I mean she's still a baby herself. Who's going to take care of them? I guess she thought with her fast tail instead of thinking with her brain, and now she's under medical care for being so stupid. Shame on her!" Co–Co's grandfather was a bit disturbed by her friend's bad judgment and he went on to ask her where Shawny's parents had been when she was going out on dates trying to be a woman. He told her he felt blessed to have such a great relationship with her. "Not only was her mother in her life, but this girl had her daddy there too, and look at her now, all knocked up and sick as ever. Now on the other hand, *you* just have lil ole me. The one who shows you love, gives you respect, and talks to you daily about real life and the uncut truth of what life is and what life could be, and as long as we continue to have heart–to–heart conversations, you are going to be all right." He nudged her with his elbow and said, "Give my five, Shorty, 'cause we are all of that, right?"

They both cracked a smile as Co–Co slapped her grandfather five. When they arrived home she noticed that the light on her caller ID box was flashing, and right away she began checking her messages. The first message was from Shawny's mother. She wanted to apologize for acting so strangely earlier. The message was quite long and her voice began to crack a little as if she was going to cry. She closed the message by saying, "LaShawn is going to pull through, and thank you so much for helping her this afternoon. I'll give you a call tomorrow."

After that, Co–Co deleted her other messages because she just didn't want to listen to any of them. She knew they were either from people calling to be nosy or from people leaving encouraging messages concerning the loss of Vicki.

After watching a little bit of television Co–Co made her way into her bedroom, where she got down on her knees, locked her hands together, and began to pray. "Father God," she said, "Please make Shawny well. I need her standing beside me, because I want her to be a part of my dedication speech to Vicki. I know you have to help a lot of people, but God, help her get well soon. In Jesus' name I pray, Amen."

The next day Co–Co had to attend the graduation rehearsal alone, without her friends. As she entered the school building she noticed just a few people lingering around the school grounds, and that was quit unusual. After the first bell rang, senior students had to report to the auditorium to rehearse. Normally she would mingle a little before taking her place in rehearsal, but for some reason she was not in the mood for socializing with her classmates. During practice, she overheard three girls sitting behind her talking softly, but they were whispering loud enough to be heard. "Ask her," one girl continuously chanted. At first Co–Co ignored them, but they kept distracting her with their whispering.

"Ask me what?" she said in a very defensive tone of voice.

"Oh… uh, Renée," one of the girls said as her voice nervously carried, "Shannon's mother is a janitor at the Kapers Hospital, and she told her that Shawny has AIDS. She said that she cleaned her room out the other night, and I was told that you were the one who had her admitted, so—"

Before she could finish her sentence, Co–Co looked at the three girls with anger in her eyes. Loudly, and in an upset manner, she shouted. "No, please…y'all people need to cut out all of that jealousy and gossiping. That girl's mother has a serious problem, because she doesn't know what she is talking about! Shawny fell out in the mall because she was overheated, that's all. She found out she was pregnant, and I guess the doctors wanted to keep her so they could make sure that she and the baby were going to be all right. The next time any of y'all have something to ask me, make sure it is not a stupid question about something ignorant like what y'all heard from some drunken maintenance woman, okay?"

The girls had dumbfounded looks upon their faces, and it was obvious to Co–Co that all three of them had hoped she would say she didn't know or that it wasn't her place to tell Shawny's business. Co–Co shook her head at them and stood up in front of them. She made her way out into the aisle, because she wanted to move away from where she was sitting. Before she left, she looked back in the direction of the three girls and chanted in a strong, sarcastic tone, "Man, where would we be today without haters in this world?"

They knew not to respond, because although she was humble, she was not a punk. So they just watched as she made her way toward another seat in the auditorium. Co–Co couldn't believe what the other girl's mother had to say about Shawny.

After attending practice, Co–Co caught the metro bus to the hospital to see Shawny. She was unable to do so. The receptionist stated that Shawny could not have visitors, only her parents were allowed to visit. *This is not right,* she thought to herself. For the life of her, she couldn't understand why the hospital was going through so much trouble to protect a pregnant teenager who had fainted. As she turned to exit the hospital, she spotted K.C. and his mother shopping in the gift shop. "I hope those balloons aren't for Shawny, because she can't have visitors—only her parents are allowed to see her."

They both looked puzzled, but without questioning Co–Co they grabbed their balloons, put their gifts into the bags, and joined Co–Co as she headed toward the exit.

Graduation was only two days away, but not once after the first message from Shawny's mother had she attempted to call Co–Co again. Co–Co was concerned and very upset, not to mention confused, about what was going on with them. At one point she suspected that what Shannon's mother had said about Shawny was true. After all, Shawny didn't call, her telephone number wasn't listed in the hospital's directory, and her visits were still off limits. Co–Co didn't want to think about Shawny in that condition, so she pushed those crazy thoughts to the back of her mind.

She began focusing on her speech for graduation, but thoughts of Vicki just popped up out of nowhere. Her concentration broken, she couldn't continue practicing because she was not one hundred percent involved in her speech. As she got up from the table, she hoped that Shawny would do something crazy and surprising like show up for graduation dressed in a matching outfit like hers. After all, that's how Shawny was, she loved attention.

After thinking about what may or may not happen, Co–Co felt focused again and resumed her speech preparations. She went over the speech about three times in the mirror and after rehearsing, she decided to call Shawny's house. No one answered, so she left a message for Shawny. The message simply said that she was becoming a bit worried. Co–Co asked why her parents were being so secretive about her fainting. She wanted Shawny to give her a call as soon as possible.

Back at Shawny's house, Shawny's mom stood in Shawny's room staring at her telephone. She had heard everything. She wanted to pick up the telephone to explain to Co–Co why her daughter wasn't released from the hospital, but she couldn't bring herself to do such a thing. She couldn't help but think to herself that in two days her daughter was supposed to graduate from high school. Shawny's mother felt very bad about being on the go all the time. She actually thought her little girl was a virgin because she had never inquired about the topic of sex. As a matter of fact, she could count on her hand how many times she and her daughter had sat down to have a general girl conversation about becoming a woman. She sadly recalled telling Shawny why young ladies had monthly cycles, and they discussed simple things like hygiene. She wished she could have been more attentive to her teenage daughter.

Somehow Shawny's parents had lost their focus of being there for her. They were too concerned with making money so their daughter could live a better life. All they stressed was school, school, school; and that was easy for Shawny, because if she brought home A's, they'd buy her nice shoes and reward her with name brand clothes. They assumed that the school would inform students of the other things they needed to know, and they thought that if she wanted to know about something that didn't pertain to school, she would have enough common sense to ask them— things like safe sex, where to get protection to prevent sexually transmitted diseases, birth control pills, etc. It was sad but true, Shawny's parents thought they knew what being responsible parents meant. Her parents now saw exactly what lack of communication could do to a child. At first it was rush, rush, rush, and everything was systematic with them when it came to going to work, paying the bills, and staying on top of their daughter's schooling. After the bad news, her parents had to face reality and deal with what was going to become a huge turning point in their lives. Something bad had happened to the daughter of two parents, whom obviously had no clue about what went on with their daughter when she stepped outside their home. Just like Vicki's mother, they allowed time to pass them by, and had to find out the hard way that being a parent meant being there for the child. That meant through the great times, and most of all, through the worst times.

Bravely, Shawny's mother picked up the telephone and dialed Co–Co's number. When Co–Co saw Shawny's telephone number displayed on the caller ID box, she immediately picked up her telephone. She asked Shawny's mom where Shawny was and how come she hadn't called her yet. "What's wrong with her? Will she be able to graduate with me?"

Before Co–Co could ask another question, Shawny's mother interrupted her. She wanted to explain to her the real reason why her daughter fainted that day in the mall. "Shawny was hiding a huge secret from me and her dad. I mean, when I say huge—I really mean enormous!"

Co–Co was afraid to ask anything after hearing her say the word 'secret'. She was certain that her mother was upset and disappointed about her pregnancy.

"Don't worry about it; she's going to be all right. We'll be there for her, so just tell her to get some rest and call me when she gets a chance."

Co–Co didn't have a clue of what Shawny's mother was getting at. She felt relieved to hear that her mother was finally coming around to accept her daughter's mistake.

"No, Renée, I don't think you understand. She went to the doctor without me, and apparently she tested positive for HIV. They gave her medication to take, but unfortunately she wasn't taking the medicine correctly and her body wasn't reacting well to the pills." Shawny's mother went on and on about how sorry she was for not being a good mother. She said that Shawny was doing much better, and that she and her husband were going to be there to support her on graduation day.

Co–Co was speechless. Her mouth flew wide open and she shut her eyes very tightly. Before hanging up the telephone, Shawny's mother thanked Co–Co for coming to support her.

Co–Co dropped to the floor in disbelief. "I told that girl to slow down. Now look at her. Please God, watch over her."

"Graduation day is finally here," her grandfather said as he did his little dance to entertain Co–Co that morning. There was a knock at the door. It was K.C., his mother, and his Aunt Lynn carrying gifts for Co–Co. K.C.'s aunt wanted her to know how proud she was of her, and she told Co–Co that a part of her felt like shutting down after the death of Vicki, but the other part told her to remain strong and be happy and thankful for a friend like her. "Not only did you motivate my baby to continue with school, you helped her become an honor roll student, and for that, sweetheart, I thank you." She hugged her and kissed her on both cheeks.

Jokingly, K.C. yelled, "Ugh... please don't give her too much, her big head might burst!"

Co–Co laughed with them and waved K.C.'s silly comment off. While entertaining Vicki's family she began to feel a little nervous, so she decided to plop down on the couch. "I'm sorry y'all. I'm not feeling too well right now. I feel queasy. Maybe I need to lie down for a little while. Thank you for everything, and I am going to represent my girl well when I give my speech today... watch and see how I roll up on dat stage!"

Before leaving, they all wished Co–Co well and assured her that they would see her later at the graduation ceremony. As soon as they left she broke into tears; she was filled with so much tension. She couldn't understand how God could bless her with the ability to be so wise and encouraging to others but take away one life and permit illness to take over her other friend's life, leaving her to watch and suffer alone.

Co–Co felt very bad. The guilt of giving Vicki her uncle's packages bothered her, the conversation she and Shawny had about her not being there for Shawny bothered her, in fact all of the things she wanted to forget bothered her. She balled herself up in her bed, threw the covers over herself, and cried like a baby. She knew her grandfather would be returning from shopping soon, so she kept her whimpering quite low because she really didn't want him to see her upset on what was supposed to be one of the happiest days of both of their lives. Since the ceremony was being held at Washington, D.C.'s Constitution Hall downtown and wasn't for another three hours, she knew she had enough time to get a little rest, shower, and once again pull herself together for the sake of her elderly, proud grandfather, who had never witnessed such an amazing event before.

After a crazy morning of dealing with her frustration, it was time for Co–Co to prepare for graduation. Her grandfather and Vicki's family members had all chipped in to purchase her an expensive pair of sunglasses so she could strut her stuff like the true diva that she was. Her hair and nails were perfect. She looked like a teenage doll. She must have washed away her sorrows during her shower, because all of her sad feelings had drained away. She felt happy and grateful that her grandfather would attend the most important day of her life. "C'mon, Granddaddy, we can't be late. We are the stars of the show, man!" She was anxious to leave, and looking good had boosted her confidence.

"Hold on, Ms. Co–Co," he said as he made a funny face at her. "I'm gonna get my camera, girl, you know you have to take a picture of the man!" He pointed to himself and gave her a confident wink.

Before snapping his picture, Co–Co jokingly yelled, "I know that's right, granddaddy... flex your stuff!"

When they arrived at the hall everyone was hugging and kissing each other. Inside, the students were all lined up, ready to make their entrance. After the students took their seats the room was filled with silence so the roll call of the graduates could begin.

Of course, Co–Co didn't have to worry about making an entrance, because she was among the ceremony's guest speakers who would sit on the stage that day.

When Co–Co's name was called, the entire auditorium roared as loud as an enormous thunderstorm. They all yelled her name and cheered her on. It was no surprise to her grandfather to hear

153

how proud everyone was of her, not to mention how popular she was. He was quite impressed, though, with the way they went wild as she made her way to the podium. After giving the audience a few moments to settle down, Co–Co took a deep breath and asked everyone to give a moment of silence for her dear friend,

Victoria Marie Carter, a.k.a. "Vicki". She then asked if she could take a few seconds to share her feelings with the entire auditorium.

"What I am about to say, may sound quite familiar to some of you. Last week I lost my best friend. I felt very sad because we were very close. The media wrote and said untrue statements about my dear friend, so today I am here to clear her name. We all knew and loved Vicki for her warm sense of humor and her creative, stylish ways. She was great and had a heart of gold. I'm sure she will be missed by all of those who were fortunate enough to know her. At first I was going to recite a poem, but I changed my mind. I didn't want this to sound rehearsed and my intentions were not to sadden this happy day. I have feelings that need to be shared from within. Victoria was murdered viciously, yet she is still alive in my heart and mind. She was an honor roll student, a dreamer, and a friend who promised me that she would stop slinging drugs soon. Unfortunately, soon wasn't soon enough, because selling drugs is what killed her. Those who knew her knew her life was a hard one to live, but she made her life easy to live every day. To all of my fellow graduates…please do not get involved with negative activity. Please take responsibility for yourselves, because I miss my friend and I don't want you or your friends to experience the loss of a loved one as Vicki's family and I did. I don't want you all to feel sorry for me, and I most definitely don't want to spoil this glorious day by adding sorrow to the program, so at this time, I would like to thank myself for doing so well and congratulate myself for being an outstanding student. Hey, look, Granddaddy! This is for you… we did it. Thank you!"

Co–Co got a standing ovation for her courageous announcement addressing her peers, but the highlight of that speech was when she issued

Vicki's diploma to her mother. Vicki's mother stepped up to the stage, reached out and grabbed her daughter's diploma, and lit up the room with her huge, pretty smile. Not only had Co–Co brightened the auditorium and her day with her outstanding stories about Vicki, for the very first time Vicki's mother' realized that she didn't need drugs to feel high, she felt so wonderful after accepting her daughter's diploma. She gained that awesome feeling once again of what it felt like to be a real parent. Although the loss of her daughter was tragic and she regretted a lot of things from her past, she was grateful to have a second chance to live her life drug–free, and to build a relationship with her other child. Before leaving the stage she sent a powerful message, and somehow she knew it had touched a lot of parents and young people in the audience. That made her feel even better.

When the name LaShawn Patrice Johnson was called, Shawny's mother walked up to accept her certificate and awards on her behalf. Before handing Shawny's mother the awards, the principal gave her an amazing introduction and mentioned how proud he was of Shawny's dedication in assisting the school's faculty association. He went on to say that he was proud of all the students and glad to see them successfully moving on. As Shawny's mother accepted the awards, thoughts of giving the audience an excuse for her daughter's absence went dancing through her head. To her it was perfect timing, because she really felt open and was willing to accept Shawny's illness now because of what Vicki's mom had said about her life story.

"First, I would like to congratulate all of you wonderful people down there wearing those caps and gowns. You are on your way to bigger and better things. Good luck. My—my daughter was unable to be here today because of health reasons. I was very proud when she asked me to accept her diploma for her, because this gives me an awesome opportunity to feel young again, not to mention graduate high school for a second time. But what's so different about it this time is I'm doing it with honors. Wow! Thank you, Mr. Long, for giving me the opportunity to accept my daughter's certificates, and once again, congratulations, class of 1999. God bless you all."

Shawny's mother's spirits were high and cheery as she joked and made fun with the audience. On the outside she appeared to be happy and filled with grace, but on the inside her heart was broken and filled with pain. She wanted to tell them the truth about her sick infected daughter because just like Vicki's mother, she was about to see for herself how it felt to lose her child. As she stepped off the stage she began to feel like a failure, because she had really wanted to tell the entire truth about why her daughter was taking medication. She honestly wanted to encourage the audience to practice safe sex or abstain from having sex until they were married. This was something that she wished she could have told her own child, and she felt bad because she knew that there had to be a lot of parents out there who weren't aware of what their teenagers were doing, because she had no idea that her daughter was sexually active at all until it was too late.

Parents and teachers began clapping and Shawny's fellow classmates were chanting her name as her mom made her way to her seat. Shawny's mother glanced across the aisle and made eye contact with Co–Co, and before she sat down she displayed an ashamed smile.

Co–Co understood why the girl's mother hadn't said anything. It was a moment of victory for the three of them, so she waved and smiled back at Shawny's mother. She continued to smile, because she couldn't believe how far she had come and she looked forward to the future. She had proved that being raised in a bad environment did not mean that a person couldn't achieve. "This is for my granddaddy," she said to the students who stood on each side of her as they made their way off the stage. When the students exited the auditorium, they were applauded for their achievements and their completion of high school. When Co–Co made her way to the lobby, she threw her hands up and shouted, "We did it, Vicki! We made it!"

After the graduation ceremony Co–Co took pictures and socialized with her schoolmates, a few of her family members, and some of her neighborhood friends who were there to support her and to attend the graduation party which was going to take place at K.C.'s house. She felt like she was on top of the world compared to the way she had been feeling earlier that morning. The day was going better than she thought it would, considering her close friends weren't there to attend the celebration.

The party was off the hook. Everybody was dancing and having a good time, until one girl walked over to Co–Co and asked her if the rumor about Shawny was true.

Defensively, she replied as she raised one eyebrow and frowned, "What... that she is pregnant and was put on bed rest, that rumor? Um–huh, it's true. Her mother is around here somewhere, why don't you ask her about her daughter? I'm quite sure that Shawny would be pleased to know you were so concerned." Co–Co walked away, leaving the girl with a dumbfounded look upon her face. She headed toward the kitchen, where Shawny's parents were preparing themselves a plate of food to take with them. "Hey,

Mr. and Mrs. Johnson are y'all going off to the hospital now, because if y'all are, I want to go, too."

"I'm sorry, Renée, but she is not doing too well, and this time of the evening she gets really cranky. I promise you, as soon as she gets a little better and she has time to adapt to the medicine, we will take you to see her, okay?"

With a closed smile, Co–Co agreed to visit Shawny when the time was right. She gave them both a hug, walked them to the front door, and saw them out. Then she joined in on the party. Everyone was dancing and singing along to the music; even her grandfather had the house jumpin'. He was dancing and singing the lyrics of rap songs and everything. The teenagers were surprised as they watched the sixty–something–year–old man spitting Jay-Z's lyrics and flowing to the Notorious B.I.G.'s "Hypnotize" song. Co–Co rocked from side to side as she watched her grandfather proudly. "Go, Granddaddy, that's right. Represent, big daddy, represent!" she shouted as she continued to watch her grandfather, who became the life of the party. K.C. and his mother got a kick out of watching him rock the party.

A couple of weeks went by and sure enough, Shawny's mother came by to pick up Co–Co to visit Shawny in the hospital. When they arrived at the hospital she asked Co–Co to wait out in the hall. She wanted to make sure that Shawny was feeling well enough for a visitor.

Understandingly, Co–Co agreed. She really didn't care whether Shawny wanted a visit or not—she planned to go into the room regardless. Not a second later she barged in the room. Anxiously, she peeped around the curtain and whispered, "I know you asked me to wait but I wanted to see her."

Apparently Shawny's parents were trying to fix her up a little. When Co–Co glanced over at her ill friend, it shocked her. Shawny was barely awake. Her eyelids seemed to get heavier with each breath she took, her hair was soft and thin as a feather and she had bald spots in the front of her head, and her lips were dry and very chapped. She had dried blood in the creases of the dry skin on her lips.

Co–Co couldn't believe how fast Shawny's body was starting to deteriorate.

When the nurse came in, Co–Co ran out. She thought she was going to be able to handle visiting her, but she couldn't. Shawny's mom went running after her. "Hey, baby, I know that it hurts to see her like that." She asked her to wait in the hall while she got her car keys so she could take her home.

During the ride home, Co–Co cried and sobbed, and after wiping her tears away, she began questioning Shawny's mother. "Mrs. Johnson, I don't understand. A couple of weeks ago she was healthy and sharp as a knife, and then all of a sudden she's weak and can barely open her eyes."

Mrs. Johnson explained what the doctors had said about her daughter's condition. She gave Co–Co all the details of what the medication was doing to Shawny's body. She thanked her for being a part of her life, and asked her to just pray for her daughter to pull through.

"Don't thank me for being a part of her life; you make it sound as if she was dead or something. You said it yourself… she'll get better, right?"

Shawny's mother smiled and squinted her eyes to hold back her tears, and before Co–Co got out of the car, she apologized. "I'm sorry that you had such a short visit with her. Maybe the next time she will be feeling up to having a visit."

Touched by what she had just witnessed, Co–Co squeezed Shawny's mother so tight and said, "It's okay. I'm her friend. I don't care how badly she feels or what she looks like. I'm always going to love her, and the next time I'm able to visit, I am going to wake her lil butt up." She closed the car door and made her way for the stairs. She felt a little relieved, because although she thought Shawny looked bad, she had pictured her looking even worse. "Whew… I'm glad she didn't have any of those ugly lesions all over her face and neck."

When Shawny's mother returned to the hospital, she spotted K.C. and his mother. Co–Co's grandfather had told them that she had gone to the hospital to visit Shawny, so they figured that Shawny was able to have visitors. How they managed to get past the sign–in officer puzzled Shawny's parents, but it was too late for anyone to turn them around because they were already entering the room.

K.C. and his mother felt very awkward looking at Shawny, so they stood there and made small talk as the doctors talked to her parents. This time she was wide-awake. They could hear her moaning as the nurse gave her medicine and fixed the dressings on her arm. K.C. couldn't help himself—he stared as she shivered and shook like an eighty-five year old women.

Shawny's mother stood beside her daughter looking very defensive. She was wondering what K.C. was thinking as he watched Shawny's reaction to the medication, because just like any mother who would protect her young, she could explain Shawny's reaction. She even described why Shawny's appearance was so bad. She told him that the day before had been much worse than what he saw today. "Boy... that stuff had her looking terrible. I'm just glad to see her finally coming around today." As she stroked her hair and tried to groom her a little bit, she noticed that K.C. had turned away to look out of the window, so she reached for a couple of wet wipes to wipe her mouth and began dabbing a little Vaseline on her lips.

Shawny squirmed and twitched a little, but eventually gave in and decided to calm herself down. The room was really quiet, when all of a sudden K.C. asked, "Where is Co–Co?"

"She just couldn't handle watching my baby this way so I took her home."

When Shawny's dad saw that pity for his family was beginning to fill the room, he jumped up and shouted, "I'm so angry, how could this happen to her? How could this be happening to us?" He went on and on about how he had raised his girl to do the right thing. As he pounded on the wall, his argument about how he had given her this and he had given her that became annoying to the whole room. What he failed to mention was that he didn't educate her about what the opposite sex would try with his little girl. Not once did he regret or admit that he was not aware of his daughter being sexually active. His attention was focused more on her grades and making sure that his car was clean. It was actually the first time that he had something to say about how he was feeling. He honestly had no one to blame for his bad parenting skills but his wife and himself.

Shawny's mother stood there sobbing. This was the first time she had heard her husband speak about Shawny's illness.

The mood was becoming very uncomfortable for K.C. and his mother, so they decided to leave, but not without saying goodbye. As they made their way across the hospital's parking lot, K.C. sarcastically said, "I knew something like that was going to happen to her. I used to see that lil girl with all types of dudes all of the time. She was as hot and fast as can be. Sometimes I used to get very angry with Vicki because she was hanging around her, and each time Vicki defended her. If she could be here to see her friend now, she would understand why I always felt that way about her."

Unaware of how fast Shawny was, K.C.'s mother felt quite sorry for Shawny's parents. "Ain't it funny how God works? Here I am alive and breathing, but my daughter is dead. I don't have a job, a car, I wouldn't have a decent place to live if my son wouldn't have accepted me back in his life, I'm broke, yet I feel proud because through all of my years of abusing drugs, I had a daughter who was surrounded by people who taught her right from wrong. I know she sold drugs, and I know she knew it was wrong, but before Vicki got killed, Co–Co told me she had planned on giving up that street life. Now, the girl Shawny…this girl had everything except the interest of her parents and that is why she's in the hospital today." She felt proud of her daughter and Co–Co, too, because they were the underdogs who had made out just fine. "I'm going to get Shawny's telephone number from Co–Co and I'm going to keep in touch with her mother because she is going to need someone to talk to."

K.C. didn't say a word. He just felt good about finally having his mother in his life. During the ride home, his mother wouldn't stop talking about how sad it was to see Shawny's diploma sitting on the cabinet near her hospital bed. It brought tears to her eyes, because she was thinking she would rather have lost her daughter the way she did than witness her dying slowly, because she just wouldn't be able to handle seeing her child that way.

When K.C. and his mother got home from the hospital, K.C. immediately phoned Co–Co. "Hello Ms. Graduate, what's going on?" Not once did he mention that he and his mother went to visit Shawny. Their conversation was about her plans for college and how proud they were of K.C.'s mother because she was doing so well. They also joked and laughed about how much fun everyone had watching her grandfather cuttin' up at the party.

After hanging up the telephone, Co–Co decided to listen to some music while she packed a few of her grandfather's things. He had decided that during summer vacation, he would search for a nice home down south in Clinton, South Carolina, where he was born and raised. Co–Co was going off to college, and what remained of his family were a few rowdy grandchildren who didn't come around unless they needed something and a daughter who was strung out on drugs and had no plans of getting herself together. It was best for him, because to him that wasn't the meaning of being a family and it wasn't worth staying around, expecting things to change. So he made a few calls down south and asked around about housing opportunities. As far as he was concerned, his job was done. He had wanted to work hard enough to pay for his granddaughter's future, and he had done just that. He had put away a lump sum of money every pay period so he would be able to afford whatever home he chose, and although he had the whole summer to enjoy being with his granddaughter before she went off to college, he thought it would be great to be prepared by packing some of his things early.

Everything was going well for them, considering the sad, dramatic changes they'd been through in the past.

After packing a few boxes, Co–Co went into the living room where she and her grandfather began to talk about her friends. She told him the truth about Vicki's lifestyle, but failed to mention anything about her role in giving Vicki those packages, and telling him about all of the money she had was definitely a no–no. She even told him the real reason why Shawny was in the hospital.

Her grandfather stood at the end of the couch with an amazed look on his face. "You are incredible, do you know that? I'm so amazed at how strong you are, and I don't care what your friends did or how bad they were, I am just glad that you were wise enough to use your own head and not be a follower." They talked and laughed about things that had happened. He even shared some of his funny moments with her, about how he grew up with a lot of knuckleheads who weren't the best peers to be around. Just because they turned out to be murderers and bank robbers didn't mean that he wanted that kind of life. He told her he was his own individual, and what they had done was teach him to be a leader, not a follower. He didn't feel the need to question her about the things her friends had gone through; instead he gave her a pat on the head and told her what an outstanding young lady she was. He compared her to her mother. "You know…you remind me so much of your momma. She was always thinking for herself, as a matter of fact out of all of my children she was the only one who didn't get hooked up into those drugs. I sure wish she could see her lil chocolate bunny hopping her way off to college."

Co–Co laughed at his little bunny joke as she made her way to the balcony. Every night she would look to the sky and find five bright stars, which she would name after her loved ones. They were her mom, her dad, her grandmother, her aunt, and her Uncle Gary. On this night she had to add two more names to the sky, Vicki and Shawny, so she went outside and took a deep breath. Although Shawny wasn't dead, she felt she was because she would never be herself again. She just considered her a rising star on her way to Heaven. "Good night, Ma, good night, Daddy." She continued to call the stars by her loved one's names. When she got to Shawny's star, Co–Co made a little joke. She smiled and said, "Shawny, stop flirting with my Uncle Gary, he is too old for you, girl." After her moment with the stars, she strolled to her bedroom to retire from another emotional day.

Two and a half months later, summer vacation was over and it was time for Co–Co and her grandfather to move on. He had found a nice three-bedroom house about four doors away from his brother. Co–Co had received her dorm information, which was subject to change as soon as she got to Atlanta. Everything was going well and she promised everyone who was close to her that she would keep in touch.

Before heading off, Co–Co wanted to stop by Shawny's to tell her goodbye, and during the ride over, she told her grandfather she was afraid to see her again. "She might look worse than she did when I saw her the first time." She wiped away the tear before it could fall down her cheek, and her grandfather reached out to comfort her.

"It's all right, Renée. C'mon now, don't get yourself all upset. Today is supposed to be a happy day

173

for us. We are not going to let this sickness get us down, okay?" He suggested that maybe it would help if she tried not to look at her too much.

As always, Co–Co got herself together. Rather than going in with her, her grandfather decided he would sit outside in his car and wait, because if she felt uncomfortable she could excuse herself by stating that she didn't want to make him wait long.

"Go ahead; I don't think I would be able to handle seeing that baby suffering like that. I'm gonna stay out here, you go on in."

When she entered the room Shawny was asleep. Her parents had transformed her room into a hospital suite. She had different breathing machines, an arrangement of pill bottles lined up across the dresser and everything else needed for an AIDS patient. Immediately Co–Co's face stiffened, because Shawny's head was completely bald and her fingernails were dark and brittle. Although she was asleep, to Co–Co, Shawny looked as if she was in a whole lot of pain judging by the frowns appearing on her face as she snored. Somehow Co–Co gained enough strength to take hold of her sick friend's hand. "Well Shawn, I'm on my way to Hot Lanta. I wish you were going with me." She rubbed her hand, and as she released it she glanced over at Shawny's diploma and the five achievement awards she had received.

Shawny's mother came into the room a few seconds later. She wanted Co–Co to take Shawny's photo album to school with her. "Renée, I don't want you to forget how gorgeous my baby was, not that anything has changed because she still is beautiful, but I want you to remember her just like this." She pointed to a picture of Shawny in the photo album. Shawny never budged. She continued to sleep heavily. Shawny's mother walked Co–Co out to the car and greeted her grandfather. They made small talk for about five minutes, but she had to end the conversation because it was time for her to administer medication through Shawny's I.V. She thanked them for coming, wished them well, and reminded Co–Co to keep in touch.

After the visit, they headed to the airport to check Co–Co's bags. They arrived very early and had some time on their hands, so Co–Co's grandfather suggested they grab a little bite to eat. During their meal he went over a few safety rules with Co–Co. "Please be careful. I don't want you to think that Atlanta, Georgia, is anything like D.C., because it's not." He told her he trusted her and he knew that her judgments would be wise ones, and after his advice and encouraging words, she responded and assured him with confidence that she wasn't going to let him down.

"Not only do you have my diploma, but just think, in a few years from now, you will have my college degree hanging right there beside it! I'm going to be all right. Remember, I told you about one of my roommates. I talked to her over the phone; she's from Forestville, Maryland, so at least I'll have somebody to talk to." She squeezed his hand and smiled continuously. She felt a little mushy on the inside because she had dreamed about this day since the beginning of her twelfth grade year. Her strong emotions were starting to show in her eyes.

Co–Co told her grandfather that she had second thoughts about going away to college, because she wanted to stay home to take care of him. He was shocked. He shook his head and stated loudly and clearly in a crazy, funny voice, "Oh…no, no, no. You betta get your lil butt on that plane and bring me home a college degree. I wish nothing but the best for you, baby. I want you to live your life and help yourself, because it's all about you, Miss Lady!"

Co–Co hugged him tightly and whispered in his ear that she loved him very much.

As usual, he had to display his coolness. "Aw c'mon girl. Turn me loose now, before you block my play with the ladies here at the airport. I don't want to get my honeys mad wit me now!"

"Yeah, right. Cut it out, Granddaddy, you are not the man."

They both laughed as they finished their meals. Soon it was time for them to head back toward the terminal gate, and as the announcement was made to board the plane, Co–Co gave her grandfather one final hug. She knew he had gone through a lot of harsh times, and was trying hard to maintain his sanity for her sake. It was the first time in her life she had seen him crying. She was speechless for a second or two, then she asked him in a joking manner if he was about to cry. "Aw... not you, Mr. Too Cool. Do I see a tear in your eye?"

With a slight sniffle, he denied it. "Nah, girl, that's sweat. It's hot in here!" They both chuckled. "I keep telling you, girl, I'm too cool for that!" he said, and as he released himself from her embrace. She promised him she would call him as soon as she got there.

Co–Co made her way toward the boarding station. Her grandfather waited around until her plane took off. He stood near the window and gazed directly at the plane as it silently backed out of the parking gate.

On the plane, Co–Co had settled into her seat, strapped on her earphones, and pulled her window shade down. As she listened to the percussion of the go–go band, the plane began to lift off. She shut her eyes and gently rocked back and forth as she got deeper and deeper into the unique style of music from the District of Columbia. "See ya, Granddaddy", she softly whispered, and the plane continued to rise higher and higher into the sky.

Her grandfather began to wave as if he heard her saying good–bye. "I'll be waiting on your return", he said, as the plane vanished into the sky. Making a tight fist, he walked away backwards and threw a punch into the air. "Yeah... my grandbaby is a college girl now, she said she would do it, and she did... she's made it happen. So long southeast, cause I'm out of here too, yeeessss!"

SOME THINGS TO

THINK ABOUT...

- Would Co-Co have made it if she did not believe in herself?

- If Co-Co trashed the drugs, do you think Vicki would have been able to continue to live her life as an average street dealer from around the way?

- Was it fair for Shawny's parents to think they were raising her correctly because she was an A student, who did not have a boyfriend and showed them normal signs of being a great daughter, despite not having discussed the facts of life with her?

· What about the handsome young teacher, who probably had the disease as well? He jeopardized the lives of his family because he violated a minor and committed rape. Although Shawny agreed to have sex with him, she was a minor and he broke the law. Do you think he was being a responsible teacher, husband or father?

· Vicki's father was an addict who obviously did not want to give up drugs to get his family back together. Do you think her mom would have stopped using drugs if Vicki would not have passed away?

· If you answered no to all of these questions then you are obviously aware of making the right choices in your life. If you think about it, Co-Co honestly didn't succeed the way she wanted to because she failed to make the right decision about giving Vicki those drugs. Now she has to start all over in a new city, in a new school, and most of all she must begin to think like a responsible young adult. I hope you have learned something from this novel. And if you know of someone who is having unprotected sex, dealing drugs or failing in school, do not turn your back on them. Give them your shoulder to lean on, and encourage them to dream big. Tell them about the struggles in this novel and compare their story to the characters in this book; and if it helps, compliment them on how well they are going to be in the future. "We are not created to fail. Failure comes from not trying to succeed."

ABOUT THE AUTHOR

Stewart graduated from Cardozo Senior High School, Washington, D.C. in 1991, attended Lemon G. Hines Jr. High School, and McGogney Elementary School, in Washington, D.C.

She is living in San Francisco, California where she is attending the Academy of Art College. Her major is Interior Architecture and Design. After school, Stewart's goal is to go into set designing for film and the television industry. The author is also in process of receiving trademark & patent rights for a pedicure slipper that she has invented, and as you can see, Stewart loves to write and visualize. When asked what inspired her to create Making It Happen, Stewart said. "I would like to start something new for the teenagers who have nothing but time on their hands after school. Today's youth are missing out on what was important to my generation and the many generations before that. A lot of teenagers don't like the situations they are in but because of their surroundings and misguided choices they are content and somehow manage to continue on with living the lifestyles of being thugs, marijuana smokers, sexually active and a high risk for catching a sexual transmitted disease, or in some cases a parent before their time. These are issues that I am concerned with because adults are not teaching these young people that they do matter and they are needed. I want to give them another avenue to take other than hip-hop music and what's the hottest gear to wear this year. I would like to see young people reading again and learning from the careless characters in my novels. In this particular novel I would also like the world to know, there are grandfathers who carry a strong role in the family too, it's not always the grandmother or as they say today… "Big Momma" who's teaching and holding the family together." There's an old saying that goes; behind every good man there's a good woman. Well, Stewart believes that behind every good woman, stands a great man.